Contents

Chapter 1: What is armed conflict?

Chapter 2: Consequences of war

Chapter 3: Intervention?

Introduction

War and Conflict is Volume 259 in the **ISSUES** series. The aim of the series is to offer current, diverse information about important issues in our world, from a UK perspective.

ABOUT WAR AND CONFLICT

In today's society, war and conflict are important issues. They permeate the daily news and media, and are always controversial topics. In this brand new addition to the **ISSUES** series, we explore the definition of armed conflict, the consequences of war and ask whether humanitarian intervention is justified or unnecessary? We also consider the human rights implications for countries at war, and look at the types of weapons involved in modern warfare.

OUR SOURCES

Titles in the **ISSUES** series are designed to function as educational resource books, providing a balanced overview of a specific subject.

The information in our books is comprised of facts, articles and opinions from many different sources, including:

⇨ Newspaper reports and opinion pieces

⇨ Website factsheets

⇨ Magazine and journal articles

⇨ Statistics and surveys

⇨ Government reports

⇨ Literature from special interest groups.

A NOTE ON CRITICAL EVALUATION

Because the information reprinted here is from a number of different sources, readers should bear in mind the origin of the text and whether the source is likely to have a particular bias when presenting information (or when conducting their research). It is hoped that, as you read about the many aspects of the issues explored in this book, you will critically evaluate the information presented.

It is important that you decide whether you are being presented with facts or opinions. Does the writer give a biased or unbiased report? If an opinion is being expressed, do you agree with the writer? Is there potential bias to the 'facts' or statistics behind an article?

ASSIGNMENTS

In the back of this book, you will find a selection of assignments designed to help you engage with the articles you have been reading and to explore your own opinions. Some tasks will take longer than others and there is a mixture of design, writing and research-based activities that you can complete alone or in a group.

FURTHER RESEARCH

At the end of each article we have listed its source and a website that you can visit if you would like to conduct your own research. Please remember to critically evaluate any sources that you consult and consider whether the information you are viewing is accurate and unbiased.

Useful weblinks

www.amnesty.org.uk

www.child-soldiers.org

www.forcedmigration.org

www.handicap-international.org.uk/schools

www.responsibilitytoprotect.org

www.oxfam.org.uk

www.ppu.org.uk

www.redcross.org.uk/education

War and Conflict

Series Editor: Cara Acred

Volume 259

Independence Educational Publishers

First published by Independence Educational Publishers

The Studio, High Green

Great Shelford

Cambridge CB22 5EG

England

© Independence 2014

British Library Cataloguing in Publication Data

War and conflict. -- (Issues ; 259)

1. War. 2. War and society. 3. Humanitarian intervention.

4. Weapons systems.

I. Series II. Acred, Cara editor of compilation.

303.6'6-dc23

ISBN-13: 9781861686701

Printed in Great Britain

MWL Print Group Ltd

Armed conflict

Where wars erupt, suffering and hardship invariably follow. Conflict is the breeding ground for mass violations of human rights including unlawful killings, torture, forced displacement and starvation.

In conflicts across the globe, governments and armed groups routinely attack civilians and commit war crimes and terrible abuses of human rights.

And yet, even in war there are rules that all sides are legally bound to obey. International humanitarian law (IHL), also known as the laws of armed conflict or the laws of war, has developed in order to mitigate the effects of such conflict. It limits the means and methods of conducting military operations. Its rules oblige combatants to spare civilians and those who no longer participate in hostilities, such as soldiers who have been wounded or have surrendered. IHL applies only during armed conflict; human rights law applies in war and peace.

But powerful nations have shown a sinister willingness to manipulate international institutions or apply double standards, often arming forces known to commit mass abuses while disclaiming responsibility for the carnage.

Although international organisations such as the United Nations have advanced in their capacity to monitor and report on human rights in conflict situations, few perpetrators of mass abuses against civilians are held accountable.

Continuing violence feeds on unresolved grievances arising from years of destructive conflict and this failure to hold perpetrators of grave abuses to account.

Amnesty International does not take sides in conflicts and has no opinion on borders. Our work in situations of armed conflict concentrates on documenting and campaigning against human rights abuses and violations of IHL, no matter who commits them.

Internal conflicts

The vast majority of armed conflicts today are internal. Many internal conflicts have persisted for decades, despite significant international efforts to find solutions.

These conflicts are often triggered by issues of identity, ethnicity, religion and competition for resources, particularly oil and mineral wealth.

In Afghanistan, the escalating conflict has resulted in death and injury to thousands of civilians. War crimes have been committed by all parties to the conflict, including international and Afghan security forces, and the Taliban.

Perpetuating violence

In Iraq, security forces are committing rather than preventing sectarian violence. The Iraqi justice system is woefully inadequate and the worst practices of Saddam Hussein's regime – torture, including rape, extra-judicial executions, unfair trials and capital punishment – continue.

There have been frequent allegations of human rights violations by US and UK soldiers but few prosecutions and convictions.

At least a dozen countries in Africa have been affected by armed conflict over the last year, despite numerous peace and international mediation processes. In all of them civilians suffered human rights abuses, and the most affected were women, children and elderly people.

What Amnesty International is doing

Amnesty International calls on all warring parties to respect IHL and human rights, and emphasises to state forces and armed groups that targeting civilians can never be justified.

Amnesty International campaigns for an end to impunity for war crimes and crimes against humanity.

We are campaigning to curb the proliferation of small arms fuelling conflict and abuses, including lobbying for the adoption of a global Arms Trade Treaty.

Amnesty International campaigns for international peacekeepers to protect civilians in Darfur and eastern Chad, and has urged its supporters across the world to write to Sudanese MPs, calling on them to take a stand against the atrocities happening in their country.

Amnesty International is also actively campaigning to end the recruitment of child soldiers and to ensure that they are demobilised and reintegrated into society.

We are lobbying the UN for strengthened protection of civilians, including strict adherence to human rights and humanitarian law in peacekeeping efforts.

Progress on accountability

The International Criminal Court (ICC) was established in 2002 to prosecute people accused of genocide, crimes against humanity and war crimes. It offers the hope that some of the perpetrators of the worst crimes committed in armed conflicts will be brought to justice. It has been hailed by governments, legal experts and civil society as the most significant development in international law since the adoption of the United Nations Charter. Amnesty International has been actively involved in all stages of the establishment of the Court.

The ICC has issued arrest warrants for people accused of war crimes and crimes against humanity committed in armed conflicts in Democratic Republic of Congo, Sudan (Darfur) and Uganda.

International tribunals established to try serious crimes committed in Former Yugoslavia, Rwanda and Sierra Leone have brought to justice leaders who have committed war crimes, crimes against humanity and genocide.

In December 2006, an overwhelming majority of states voted at the UN General Assembly to consider the question of a universal and legally binding Arms Trade Treaty, a landmark step towards greater accountability of the arms trade.

⇨ The above information is reprinted with kind permission from Amnesty International. Please visit www.amnesty.org or www.amnesty.org.uk/arms for further information.

Note: In April 2013, 156 countries at the UN General Assembly voted to adopt a universal and legally binding Arms Trade Treaty, a landmark step towards regulating the multi-million dollar arms trade and saving lives. By September, more than 100 states including the United States, the world's largest arms dealer, had signed the treaty which comes into force as soon as 50 states have legally ratified it.

World religions: war and peace

Many wars have been fought with religion as their stated cause, and with peace as their hoped-for end.

What follows is a very brief summary of what the world's major religions say about war – and peace. Of course, religious beliefs are often complicated; individuals and groups within each religion have different views and religious affiliation is often closely associated with partisan emotions.

A summary can only give a very limited picture. But it can open a door to understanding the links between religion and war.

War: wrong, just or holy?

Put simply, there are three possible views of war that a religion might adopt.

The pacifist view: all violence and killing is wrong.

Belief in a 'Just War': some wars, at least, are right because they are perceived to be in the interests of justice – and should therefore be fought according to just rules.

Belief in 'Holy War': the God of a religion is perceived to ask, or command, its followers to make war on those who do not believe in that religion and who pose a threat to those who do.

Supporting non-violence

Three major world religions have their roots in India: Hinduism, Buddhism and Sikhism. Buddhism and Sikhism both grew from Hinduism. All three share the idea of non-violence (ahimsa).

The term 'non-violence' was actually coined in English (about 1920) by Mohandas Karamchand Gandhi (1869–1948) as a direct translation of 'ahimsa', 'avoiding harm to others'. The idea of non-violence was very important to Mahatma Gandhi's thinking and actions as a Hindu leader during India's approach to independence in 1947. He wrote:

'I object to violence because when it appears to do good, the good is only temporary; the evil it does is permanent.'

Hinduism

Hinduism is perhaps the oldest world religion; in some of its writings, ahimsa has been considered the highest duty from the beginning of time. Jainism also grew out of Hinduism; Jainists believe that people should strive to become detached from the distractions of worldly existence; and that the practice of ahimsa is an essential step on the way to personal salvation.

In Hinduism, however, there is another tradition. The Hindu scripture called the 'Bhagavad Gita' tells the story of Arjuna, who learns it is his duty to fight as a member of the soldier caste. Arjuna is told by his chariot driver Krishna, who is really the god Vishnu in human form, that:

'Even without you, all the soldiers standing armed for battle will not stay alive. Their death is foreordained.' Bhagavad Gita 11:32 – 3.

In the story Arjuna overcomes his doubts and fights, even though he knows it means killing some of his own family. Strict rules, however, are laid down for war: cavalry may only go into action against cavalry, infantry against infantry and so on. The wounded, runaways and all civilians are to be respected. The idea of a Just War is represented here.

How did Gandhi deal with this story in a scripture he loved? He thought of it as an allegory, and interpreted it as meaning that one should certainly engage in struggle, but only by means of non-violence. Certainly one should not kill anyone. However, not all Hindus interpret the story in Gandhi's way.

Buddhism

'Hatred is never appeased by hatred in this world; it is appeased by love.' (Dhammapada I 5).

Buddhism developed from the teaching of Siddhartha Gautama, called the Buddha (c.563–483 BC), who believed that human suffering could be overcome by following a particular way of life. The first precept of Buddhism is 'non-harming' (ahimsa): Buddhists reject violence. Buddhism is clearly pacifist in its teaching, and many Buddhists say quite bluntly that it is 'better to be killed than to kill'. Some Buddhists have been very active in promoting peace, particularly during the Vietnam War (1961–1975), when they offered a 'Third Way' of reconciliation between the American and Communist armies. Some Buddhist monks burned themselves to death in self-sacrificing protest against the war.

Buddhism perhaps has the best record of all religions for non-violence. However, Buddhists in Sri Lanka have been criticised for oppressing the Tamil minority there (Tamils are a mostly Hindu people whose origins are in southern India).

Buddhism, like all religions, seeks to be ethical. Confucianism and Taoism, which both developed in China, also share similar principles with Buddhism. For example, they seek to adjust human life to the inner harmony of nature (Confucianism) and emphasise mediation and non-violence as means to the higher life (Taoism). The founders of these religions, Confucius and Lao-Tsze, lived in the same period as Buddha, the 6th century BC.

Sikhism

Guru Nanak (1469–1534), the first Sikh Guru (a guru is a spiritual teacher, a revered instructor) wrote this hymn:

'No one is my enemy

No one is a foreigner

With all I am at peace

God within us renders us

Incapable of hate and prejudice.'

He too emphasised the importance of non-violence and the equality of all humans whatever their religion (he was particularly concerned to reconcile Hinduism and Islam). But this pacifist emphasis changed as persecution against the Sikhs developed. The sixth Guru said:

In the Guru's house, religion and worldly enjoyment should be combined – the cooking pot to feed the poor and needy and the sword to hit oppressors.

The tenth and last Guru, Guru Gobind Singh (1666–1708) was a general as well as a Guru. In order to strengthen the courage and military discipline of the Sikhs at a time of great persecution, he organised the Khalsa – the Sikh brotherhood. Guru Gobind Singh expressed the idea of 'Just War' as follows:

'When all efforts to restore peace prove useless and no words avail,

Lawful is the flash of steel. It is right to draw the sword.'

But the idea of 'Holy War' is not found in Sikhism. A central teaching of Sikhism is respect for people of all faiths.

Holy warriors

Three world religions with their roots in the Middle East adopted, at some stages of their history, the idea of a 'Holy War', as well as that of a 'Just War'.

Judaism

'They shall beat their swords into ploughshares and their spears into pruning hooks: nation shall not lift up sword against nation, neither shall they learn war any more' (The Old Testament: Isaiah 2:4).

Peace is the central teaching of rabbinical Judaism (teachings based on the writings of early Jewish scholars). However, Judaism is not a pacifist religion. The idea of Holy War occurs in the Hebrew Bible, but it was not about making others Jewish, but about survival.

The idea of 'Just War' is clearly expressed both in the Old Testament (see Deuteronomy 20:10–15,19–20) and in the later rabbinical tradition.

So while revenge and unprovoked aggression are condemned, self-defence is justified. Jews have been victims of dreadful persecution, usually at the hands of Christians, for nearly 2,000 years, culminating in the Holocaust during the Second World War (1939–1945). On the other hand, defending modern Israel and dealing justly with the Palestinians places thoughtful Jews in difficult dilemmas.

Christianity

Christianity, during its 2,000-year history, has taken up all three positions on war: Pacifism, Just War and Crusade or Holy War. Jesus' teachings in the Sermon on the Mount (The New Testament: Matthew 5–7) are very clearly non-violent: for example, 'blessed are the peacemakers, for they shall be called the children of God' (Matthew 5:9) and 'love your enemies' (Matthew 5:44).

Pacifism was the teaching and practice of the Christian Church until the Roman Emperor Constantine (274–337) made Christianity the official religion of the Empire. Pacifism then largely gave way to the development of the 'Just War' doctrine. Politics and religion were able to endorse each other in going to war.

In the Middle Ages the Crusades were fought mainly to recover the Holy Land (the area between the Mediterranean and the River Jordan) from Muslim rule. Today most Christians would be ashamed of the terrible cruelty and injustice to which the Crusades gave rise. Most Christians would also be ashamed of the later persecution of heretics (people who did not accept the official teachings of the Christian church) and non-Christians (such as Jews).

The majority of present-day Christians support the idea that war is regrettable but unavoidable and should be fought according to 'Just War' rules. Pacifism is a minority position held by some Christians in the larger denominations (Roman Catholic, Church of England, Methodist, etc.). The Quakers, Mennonites, Amish and Hutterites

together make up the historical 'peace churches', with a long tradition of pacifist belief and action.

The question remains: which position on war is the most faithful to the teaching of Jesus, who advised his followers to 'turn the other cheek' and who, when arrested, forbade a disciple to use a sword?

Islam

'Islam' means 'submission' or 'surrender' to the will of God (Allah). Its founder was the prophet Mohammed (c.570–632), who recorded his understanding of the word of Allah in the Islamic sacred book, the Qur'an.

Islamic teaching is often misunderstood in the West, particularly on the matter of Jihad. What does Jihad mean? One scholar wrote: 'Jihad means to 'strive' or 'struggle' in the way of God' Jihad has two further meanings:

⇨ the duty of all Muslims, as individuals and as a community, to exert themselves to realise God's will, to lead good lives, and to extend the Islamic community through such things as preaching and education, and:

⇨ 'Holy War' for, or in defence of, Islam.

In the West Jihad has retained only the meaning of 'Holy War'.

However, it is more correct to say that there are four different kinds of Jihad:

⇨ personal spiritual and moral struggle in order to overcome self-centredness and follow the teachings of the Qur'an;

⇨ calm preaching;

⇨ righteous behaviour that witness to the unbeliever about the way of Islam; and

⇨ war against those who oppress or persecute believers.

All faithful Muslims are thus involved in a continuous 'greater jihad' which is largely non-violent. 'The lesser jihad', war, is commanded by Allah but must be carried out according to strict rules.

There is a sense in which the lesser jihad is both 'Holy War' and 'Just War'. But it is not about making others Muslim, although some Muslims believe it is. The Qur'an says: 'There shall be no compulsion in religion.'

One Muslim became widely known for his practice of non-violence. Abdul Gaffar Khan, a member of the often warlike Pathans on the north-west frontier of India, adopted Gandhi's ideas in leading his people to independence with the establishment of Pakistan. He became known as 'the Frontier Gandhi'. Like Gandhi, he was often imprisoned.

The humanist view

In recent times religion has played a decreasing role in many societies, particularly in the West. Many people have consciously rejected the notion of a spiritual and sacred religion or god. This does not necessarily mean the rejection of ethical principles. Some people have developed a philosophy of 'humanism'. This is based on humanitarian ideals, such as individual responsibility for one's actions, respect for others, co-operating for the common good and sharing resources.

Some humanists would accept the 'Golden Rule', a term first used by Confucius: 'Do as you would be done by', or 'Treat others as you would wish them to treat you'. Some see the natural or logical conclusion of such a principle to be the rejection of all war and violence. Others, who have reservations about pacifism, argue for 'Just War' rules similar to those based on religious law.

Pacifism

The Peace Pledge Union campaigns against war and promotes peace. We challenge the values and attitudes which are a serious obstacle to action for peace. As a non-sectarian organisation we welcome co-operation with a variety of other groups, religious or non-religious, who share our aims.

'I object to violence because when it appears to do good, the good is only temporary; the evil it does is permanent.'

Was Gandhi right?

⇨ The above information is reprinted with kind permission from the Peace Pledge Union. Please visit www.ppu.org.uk/learn/learnstudy/world_religions.html for further information.

Armed conflicts decreased in 2012, but fatalities increased

Last year the number of armed conflicts decreased markedly, at the same time as the number of battle-related deaths in these conflicts increased dramatically, largely due to the situation in Syria. This is described by peace researchers at Uppsala University's Conflict Data Program (UCDP) in an article recently published in the *Journal of Peace Research*.

UCDP registered 32 active armed conflicts in 2012, which is a reduction by five since the year before. Despite this the total number of battle-related deaths increased dramatically during the year. Only at six times in the 24 years that have passed since the end of the Cold War has UCDP reported higher levels.

'It is mostly the war in Syria that has caused this large increase,' Lotta Themnér, one of the UCDP project leaders, says. 'Not since the end of the interstate war between Eritrea and Ethiopia in 1999–2001 have we seen a conflict this bloody.'

Despite this, relatively little has been done by the international community.

'This is remarkable since all large conflicts since the mid-1980s have seen close collaboration between the major powers to find, at a minimum, a ceasefire between the parties, but oftentimes also a negotiated settlement. It does not bode well for the future development of major power relations, and this in turn will affect how local conflicts are handled,' says Professor Peter Wallensteen, leader of the Program.

Aside from the war in Syria, developments in some other major conflicts also contributed to the gloomy numbers. In Somalia and Yemen violence escalated and fatalities increased markedly.

After a three-year period where few peace processes reached a negotiated settlement, the number of peace agreements increased in 2012. During the year four accords were signed: one each in the Central African Republic, South Sudan and the Philippines, and also one in the conflict between South Sudan and Sudan. Even if this number is positive news at a first glance, the researchers add that this needs to be seen in a larger context. The conflicts are still plentiful and the amount of concluded agreements remains well below the level of the 1990s. Furthermore, the signing of an agreement is only a first step in a long process towards peace and many of the accords have already reached an impasse.

7 January 2013

⇨ The above information is reprinted with kind permission from Uppsala Conflict Data Program and Uppsala University, July 2013. Please visit www.pcr.uu.se/about/news_archive/#jpr for further information.

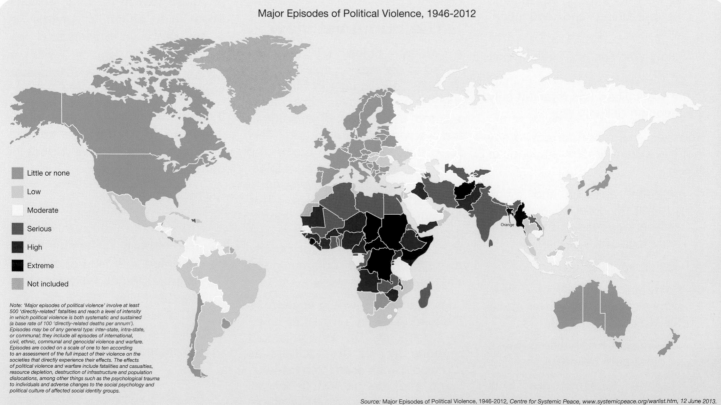

Major Episodes of Political Violence, 1946-2012

Little or none
Low
Moderate
Serious
High
Extreme
Not included

Orange

Note: 'Major episodes of political violence' involve at least 500 'directly-related' fatalities and reach a level of intensity in which political violence is both systematic and sustained (a base rate of 100 'directly-related deaths per annum'). Episodes may be of any general type: inter-state, intra-state, or communal; they include all episodes of international, civil, ethnic, communal and genocidal violence and warfare. Episodes are coded on a scale of one to ten according to an assessment of the full impact of their violence on the societies that directly experience their effects. The effects of political violence and warfare include fatalities and casualties, resource depletion, destruction of infrastructure and population dislocations, among other things such as the psychological trauma to individuals and adverse changes to the social psychology and political culture of affected social identity groups.

Source: Major Episodes of Political Violence, 1946-2012, Centre for Systemic Peace, www.systemicpeace.org/warlist.htm, 12 June 2013.

Laws of war

Even in times of war, there are rules.

What exactly is a war crime? Who decides what is legal during a conflict? How are suspects brought to justice? This short briefing cannot give full answers. But it is a useful start to understanding the principles of what are sometimes called the laws of war or armed conflict, and sometimes international humanitarian law.

Who says what is or isn't legal in war?

Modern-day laws mostly date back to the middle of the 19th century, with significant developments and additions throughout the 20th century. They are described more fully below. But it would be wrong to think that having rules about war is a modern invention.

Ancient civilisations had codes of war. The Roman republic thought about what was and wasn't a 'Just War'. The chivalric codes of medieval Europe may have been romanticised by later writers, yet they clearly indicate that medieval knights had a sense of the ethics of fighting. Ideas about the correct treatment of prisoners and behaviour during siege warfare, for example, were discussed and formulated.

Do the laws identify who is guilty of starting any particular war?

It is good to separate out two important ideas. The first covers what happens once a conflict has started, and looks at actions of the combatants, treatment of prisoners, help for the wounded and so on. This is known by the legal Latin phrase *jus in bello*. It is what soldiers mean by the 'laws of armed conflict' and what lawyers and humanitarians tend to call 'international humanitarian law'.

Another phrase, *jus ad bellum*, covers the 'who started it and why?' questions. This briefing will not deal much with this area of the law. It can be summed up as wars are illegal – which is what the United Nations charter more or less says. But it adds that every nation has the right to self-defence. The UN Security Council can authorise military action to restore international peace and security. How this works out in practice can be highly political and far from easy to resolve. The international community hopes to agree a definition of the crime of aggression – which is a quick way of getting to the heart of the 'who started it?' question. But at the moment, there is no agreement and discussions may take many more years.

What is the point of laws about war?

Quite simply, to save lives and reduce suffering. Wars are terrible. Avoiding them at all costs is best. But when they happen, the actions of the combatants can make a big difference to the lives of those involved. If prisoners are taken, treated humanely and allowed to send messages to their families, the suffering

is reduced. The same applies if weapons inflict no more injury than is militarily necessary. Likewise, if medical help can be brought to the wounded without interference and if civilians are protected. These are all covered by international humanitarian law, as the laws of war are known.

Is the Geneva Convention part of international humanitarian law?

Yes, that familiar phrase that comes to many people's mind is very much central. But it is not the full story. There is more than one Geneva Convention – and there are other laws, such as the laws of The Hague and various international treaties that are all part of international humanitarian law.

A quick summary of the legal agreements about how wars are fought would go like this:

The first international treaty to protect military victims of warfare on land was drawn up and signed in 1864 in Geneva. It was the result of action by Henry Dunant, a Swiss businessman who founded the International Committee of the Red Cross, which still plays a unique role in international humanitarian law.

Most European states that were around at the time signed it. Then at a conference in 1899, international protection was extended to wounded, sick and shipwrecked members of armed forces at sea. In 1929, a further convention was adopted specifically to help protect prisoners of war.

In 1949, these Conventions were updated and a fourth was added. They are known as the Geneva Conventions and all four are still in force today. Each deals with the protection and humane treatment of different categories of people who are no longer taking part in hostilities or who never were. They are injured soldiers, injured members of the armed forces at sea, prisoners of war and civilians.

What other significant treaties are there?

The Hague Conventions, significant ones dating from 1899 and 1907, tend to cover military tactics and the weapons that can be used. Another Hague Convention from 1954 gave protection under law to cultural property – making it a crime to attack significant art works, museums, libraries, historical monuments and similar cultural artefacts.

More recently, there have been three 'additional protocols' to the 1949 Geneva Conventions. In 1977, Protocol I gave additional protection to victims of international armed conflicts and Protocol II gave protection to victims of non-international armed conflicts. Then in 2005 the third additional Protocol provided for an additional protective emblem – the red crystal, alongside the red cross and red crescent.

But that's not all. There have also been protocols or conventions prohibiting the production and use of chemical weapons, anti-personnel mines and laser blinding weapons, among others.

Why have these laws evolved over such a long period?

Partly because they are complicated and take a lot of negotiating and clarification to reach agreement. Even now, countries can 'opt out' of specific aspects of the agreement they do not agree with.

Laws also need to develop to keep up with changes in weapons and military tactics. One of the early conventions prohibited the 'launching of projectiles and explosives from balloons'. That was in 1899 and balloons were important then. Similarly, after World War I agreements were reached prohibiting the use of 'asphyxiating, poisonous or other gases'.

There was no law specifically against genocide during the first half of the 20th century. It was only after World War II that lawyers came together to define it and prohibit it as one of the gravest of all crimes.

More recently, it can be seen that laws have also had to respond to the changing nature of warfare. The great emphasis in the early days of international humanitarian law was on conflicts between nations, fought by soldiers on battlefields. But many of today's armed conflicts are within states. They are not necessarily fought by identifiable armies, but by groups variously labelled guerrillas, rebels or insurgents. It is not always easy to see how rules devised about, say, prisoners of war fit modern circumstances.

Are all breaches of international humanitarian law regarded as war crimes?

No. The phrase 'war crime' is generally used to mean 'a grave breach' or serious violation of the Geneva Conventions or other laws and customs of war. That can include wilful killing, torture or inhumane treatment, taking hostages, killing prisoners, attacks on undefended towns which are not military objectives, or attacks on civilians or on those who are providing humanitarian assistance.

So attacking a hospital marked with a red cross is likely to be a war crime. Refusing to allow the International Committee of the Red Cross access to prisoners may be a technical breach of the laws of armed conflict, but probably would not constitute a war crime.

Do those suspected of breaches of international humanitarian law ever go on trial?

Yes. The judicial process is broadly the same as for any other criminal trial – starting with an indictment, presentation of evidence, examination and cross-examination of witnesses. National courts can try alleged breaches, and often such cases are heard by a court martial. In recent years special tribunals have been set up, such as those following conflicts in Rwanda and in the former republic of Yugoslavia.

There is now an International Criminal Court in The Hague which can and does prosecute if for any reason a country is unable or unwilling to investigate and try people suspected of war crimes in their own national courts.

Discussion and activity ideas:

⇨ Find examples of how the laws of war have reduced suffering. Research particular areas, such as protection of civilians, care of prisoners or medical assistance. How did the law help people? How much worse might things have been if there were no laws?

⇨ Some politicians and commentators have said that the Geneva Conventions are outdated and need a complete overhaul to suit modern conflicts. Why might people say this? What kinds of wars are they thinking about? Discuss differences between wars now and those of the 19th or early 20th century. Are civilians affected differently? Look at whether combatants are recognisable or not, whether they wear uniforms and act under orders. Do you think that entirely new rules are needed?

⇨ Not enough people are aware of what the laws of armed conflict are. Soldiers in a regular army are likely to be instructed and drilled in the basics, and commanded by officers who have access to legal advisers. But those instructions may not be available in poorer countries of the world, or to young people who have been forcibly recruited into a militia. Invite students to think through the problems. How might the laws of war be better known?

⇨ The above information is reprinted with kind permission from the British Red Cross. Please visit www.redcross.org.uk/education for further information.

Note: The British Red Cross is a neutral and impartial organisation. It does not engage in controversies of a political, racial, religious or ideological nature.

© The British Red Cross 2013

Landmines

Antipersonnel landmines are explosive devices designed to injure or kill people.

They are placed under, on, or near the ground, where they lie hidden for years or even decades until a person or an animal sets them off. Landmines cannot be aimed; they kill and wound indiscriminately, posing a severe risk to civilian populations, peacekeepers and aid workers long after a conflict has ended.

Antipersonnel landmines were used systematically in international and internal conflicts from the Second World War onwards. Originally intended to protect anti-tank minefields from removal by enemy soldiers, the weapons were designed to maim rather than kill an enemy soldier, with the idea that more resources are taken up on the battlefield in caring for an injured soldier than dealing with a dead soldier.

Due to their low cost and high effectiveness, landmines became increasingly used around the world. From the 1970s onwards they were used as offensive weapons to terrorise civilian populations, denying communities access to their farmland and restricting population movement.

The vast majority of landmine victims are civilians

Year after year, the Landmine Monitor has reported that civilians account for 70 to 85 per cent of casualties. Landmines are still killing and maiming ordinary people every day. This is not just during a conflict – most of the countries where casualties are reported are no longer at war.

Thanks to the 1997 Mine Ban Treaty, landmine use has dramatically dropped in recent years and although some countries are still producing them, the global trade has almost entirely halted. However, over 75 countries and territories around the world are affected by landmines and/or explosive remnants of war. The weapon poses a significant and lasting threat to communities around the world living in contaminated areas.

How do they work?

Made up of a quantity of explosive contained in a fuse body with a detonation mechanism, landmines are set off by the victims themselves, causing serious injury or death. More than 360 models have been manufactured, in two main categories:

Blast mines

Triggered by direct pressure on the mine (1–7 kg) they are designed to destroy an object at close proximity. They are primarily designed to amputate the victim's lower limbs.

Fragmentation mines

Triggered by pressure, traction or tripwires. They are designed to kill or injure individuals or groups of people. Most of these mines have a metal body which breaks into a shower of fragments when they explode. Others contain metal balls or fragments which turn into lethal projectiles in the explosion.

There are three main categories of fragmentation mines:

Fixed directional effect mines

The balls or metal shards contained in the mine are projected horizontally at an angle of 60° and at a height of over two metres causing serious or even fatal injuries over a distance of up to 50 metres.

Area effect bounding mines

When the mine is triggered, a propelling charge lifts the mine approximately 1.5 metres above the ground, then the main charge ignites. The balls or metal shards within the mine are projected over a minimum radius of 25 metres at an angle of 360°, killing within a range of 35 metres or more and causing serious injury at a distance of over 100 metres.

Fixed area effect stake mines

Metal fragments from the body of the mine are projected at an angle of 360° killing within a radius of four metres and causing serious injuries well beyond this distance.

⇨ The above information is reprinted with kind permission from Handicap International. Please visit www.handicap-international.org.uk/schools for further information.

Image © Handicap International

© Handicap International 2013

Countering weapons proliferation

Information from the Foreign & Commonwealth Office.

The Chemical Weapons Convention

The UK is one of 188 countries that have ratified the Chemical Weapons Convention (CWC), the first arms-control treaty to introduce a verifiable ban on an entire class of weapons of mass destruction (WMD).

The CWC entered into force on 29 April 1997 and all Member States must agree to its provisions, which include:

⇨ to chemically disarm by destroying all stockpiles of chemical weapons, any facilities which produced them and any old or abandoned chemical weapons from the past;

⇨ never to develop, produce, stockpile or use chemical weapons;

⇨ submit regular declarations to the Organisation for the Prohibition of Chemical Weapons (OPCW) on the production, processing, consumption, and import and export of certain dual-use chemicals;

⇨ allow the OPCW to carry out routine inspections on their territories.

The OPCW is based in The Hague, and has the mandate to achieve the object and purpose of the CWC, which includes an international verification regime to build confidence between CWC States Parties.

Restricting the development of nuclear weapons

Under the Nuclear Non-Proliferation Treaty, non-nuclear weapon states agree not to acquire or develop nuclear weapons and to prevent the spread of nuclear weapons. This includes accepting international verification of their nuclear programmes by the International Atomic Energy Agency (IAEA). States that have nuclear weapons (China, France, Russia, UK and US) agree to work towards nuclear disarmament.

The UK is working to ensure nuclear material and technology can be shared for peaceful purposes. Part of this work seeks to minimise the risk of countries that do not have nuclear weapons misusing technology and material to develop the capability to create nuclear weapons. Specifically, we support:

⇨ stronger powers for the International Atomic Energy Agency;

⇨ stronger compliance mechanisms and procedures to ensure that Iran and North Korea comply with their international obligations;

⇨ the principle and practice of nuclear weapons free zones, including the call for a Middle East zone free of nuclear weapons as well as other WMD.

We also recommend immediate discussions at the UN Security Council if a country announces its intention to withdraw from the Nuclear Non-Proliferation Treaty.

We continue to make the case for all states to sign and ratify the Comprehensive Test Ban Treaty which bans nuclear explosions by everyone, everywhere; and to begin negotiations on a Fissile Material Cut-off Treaty (a global ban on the production of fissile material for nuclear weapons and other nuclear explosive devices) within the Conference on Disarmament.

Embargoes and sanctions

Sanctions are measures by which the international community targets certain countries, individuals and/or entities to coerce them into changing their behaviour so that they will no longer threaten international peace and security, abuse human rights or act contrary to international norms and/or obligations.

They can include arms embargoes, travel bans, asset freezes, reduced diplomatic links, reduction in any military relationship, suspension from international organisations, withdrawal of aid, trade embargoes and restriction on cultural/sporting links.

The European Union applies sanctions or restrictive measures in pursuit of the specific objectives of the Common Foreign and Security Policy (CFSP) as set out in Article 11 of the Treaty on European Union.

The use of United Nations mandatory sanctions is intended to apply pressure on a state or entity to comply with the objectives set by the Security Council without resorting to the use of force. Sanctions thus offer the Security Council an important instrument to enforce its decisions.

The UK has trade and financial sanctions against a number of states as a result of the UK's foreign policy commitments and the imposition of EU and UN sanctions and embargoes.

The detailed guide *Current arms embargoes and other restrictions* lists the countries subject to controls and describes the sanctions that have been imposed and any stricter trade controls that are in place.

19 August 2013

⇨ The above information is reprinted with kind permission from the Foreign & Commonwealth Office. Please visit www.gov.uk for further information.

Chemical export licences for Syria – just another UK deal with a dictator

Britain is in no position to lecture on human rights when Vince Cable's authorisation follows a long history of arms sales.

By Nick Dearden

The latest revelations about the authorisation of chemical exports to Syria proves that British ministers should avoid two things – lecturing the public on personal morality and lecturing the world on human rights. Both will come back to bite them. While Nick Clegg commented on the pages of *The Guardian* earlier this year that the UK was a 'beacon for human rights', his business secretary was authorising companies to sell chemicals capable of being used to make nerve gas to a country in the middle of a civil war.

Clegg almost certainly knew nothing about the potential sales, and indeed the sales themselves might have been quite innocent, but our history should tell us that precaution is the best principle. If the companies had got their act together to ship the goods to Syria, they would probably have received government support through a unit of Cable's Department for Business, Innovation and Skills, called UK Export Finance. This unit has sold weapons to some of the worst dictators of the past 40 years – and had a role to play in the most serious chemical weapons abuses since the Vietnam war.

Jubilee Debt Campaign has released new information which confirms that the British Government effectively armed both sides during the Iran-Iraq war – one of the Middle East's most bloody conflicts.

Britain had been happily selling weapons to Saddam Hussein, our ally during his war against the new Islamic Republic, in the early 1980s. The UK Government also allowed the sale of the goods needed to make a chemical plant which the US later claimed was essential to Saddam's chemical weapons arsenal, with the full knowledge that the plant was likely to be used to produce nerve gas. Saddam used chemical weapons against Iranian soldiers and against civilians within his own country in 1988, killing tens of thousands.

This is old news, but we now also know that until the fall of the Shah in 1979, Britain also sold Rapier missiles and Chieftain tanks to Iran's autocratic regime – weapons that were undoubtedly also used in the Iran-Iraq war.

Both sets of arms were effectively paid for by the British taxpayer, as both Iraq and Iran defaulted on the loans given by Britain, and they became part of Iraq and Iran's debt. Though Iran still 'owes' £28 million to Britain, plus an undisclosed amount of interest, this did not stop Britain guaranteeing £178 million of loans to Iran to buy British exports for gas and oil developments in the mid-2000s, thus breaking its own rules.

This new information adds to a litany of such cases – supporting arms sales to the brutal General Suharto of Indonesia, both Sadat and Mubarak in Egypt and military juntas in Ecuador and Argentina, the latter using its British weapons to invade the Falkland Islands.

In opposition, Cable railed against the use of taxpayer money to support such sales, and his party promised to audit and cancel these debts and stop the sales. In power, he behaves the same way as his predecessors. While regularly claiming such deals are a 'thing of the past', Cable has signed off £2 billion of loans to the dictatorship in Oman to buy British Typhoon fighter aircraft, the sale of a hovercraft to the highly indebted Pakistan navy and an iron ore mine in Sierra Leone which has not even been assessed for its human rights impact.

Cable has ripped up Liberal Democrat policy to keep on supporting the sale of dangerous goods. He continues to insist on the repayment of debts run up by the UK selling weapons to now deposed dictators. Far from being a beacon for human rights, the UK has little legitimacy around the world when it comes to taking sides in wars – a fact that Parliament recognised in its welcome vote last Thursday.

Next week, Britain's true role in the world will be on show in Docklands – when the world's 'leading' military sales event meets in London. As war and the aftermath of war still rage across the Middle East, one way we as citizens improve our country's damaged reputation is to protest against such an appalling expression of Britain's role in the world. Authorising the export of chemicals to Syria is simply part of a long trend of support for dangerous technology which undermines this country's legitimacy when it comes to speaking about human rights.

2 September 2013

⇨ The above information is reprinted with kind permission from *The Guardian*. Please visit www.guardian.co.uk for further information.

'Killer robots' which are able to identify and kill targets without human input should be banned, UN urged

Human rights investigator Christof Heyns to lead calls against lethal robotic weapons.

The UN Human Rights Council will be warned of the ethical dangers posed by so-called 'killer robots'; autonomous machines able to identify and kill targets without human input.

Tonight's talk in Geneva will include an address by Christof Heyns – the UN special rapporteur on extrajudicial, summary or arbitrary executions for the Office of the High Commissioner for Human Rights – who will call for a moratorium on such technology to prevent their deployment on the battlefield.

Heyns, has submitted a 22-page report on 'lethal autonomous robots', says that the deployment of such robots 'may be unacceptable because no adequate system of legal accountability can be devised' and because 'robots should not have the power of life and death over human beings'.

Heyns, a South African law professor who fulfils his role independently for the UN, has highlighted in particular the US's counter-terrorism operations using remotely-piloted drones to target individuals in hotspots such as Pakistan and Yemen.

Although fully autonomous weapons have not yet been developed Heyns says that 'there is reason to believe that states will, inter alia, seek to use lethal autonomous robotics for targeted killing'.

Heyns points to the history of drone-deployment as evidence that countries could escalate to using autonomous robots. Drones were originally intended only for surveillance purposes and 'offensive use was ruled out because of the anticipated adverse consequences'.

These considerations were ignored once it had been established that weaponised drones could provide 'advantage over an adversary'.

The report highlights that despite recent advances, current military technology is still 'inadequate' and unable 'to understand context'. This makes it difficult for robots to establish whether 'someone is wounded and *hors de combat*' or 'in the process of surrendering'.

Heyns added that 'A further concern relates to the ability of robots to distinguish legal from illegal orders.'

'The UN report makes it abundantly clear that we need to put the brakes on fully autonomous weapons, or civilians will pay the price in the future,' said Steve Goose, arms director at Human Rights Watch. 'The US and every other country should endorse and carry out the UN call to stop any plans for killer robots in their tracks.'

Barack Obama defended drone use in a speech last Friday, arguing that the use of unmanned aerial vehicles (UAVs) was not only legal but the most efficient way of targeting terrorists. He referenced the 'heartbreaking' civilian casualties caused by their use, but said that armed intervention was more dangerous – both for civilians and soldiers.

Examples of autonomous weapons systems already in use include the US Navy's Phalanx gun system that automatically engages incoming threats and the Israeli Harpy drone that automatically attacks radar emitters.

29 May 2013

⇨ The above information is reprinted with kind permission from *The Independent*. Please visit www.independent.co.uk for further information.

WOW! THAT'S A SCARILY REALISTIC GAME!

IT ISN'T A GAME!

Drones could replace peacekeepers in Ivory Coast

Ivory Coast asks UN to consider using unmanned drones when peacekeeping forces are reduced later this year.

By Afua Hirsch

Peacekeepers in Ivory Coast could be replaced by drones in a further step towards greater use of the military aircraft in sub-Saharan Africa.

Ivory Coast, whose security situation is described as 'fragile' after a decade of turmoil that culminated in a brief civil war in 2011, has asked the United Nations to consider deploying the unmanned aerial systems when its peacekeeping forces are reduced later this year.

'The use of drones would enhance the monitoring capacity of the UN mission in Ivory Coast, especially its surveillance and information gathering,' said Sylvie van den Wildenberg, spokesperson for the UN Operation in Ivory Coast (UNOCI).

'This would help us to cope better with the difficulty we face in the west of the country and the heavily forested border area with Liberia, which is very difficult to monitor and an ideal sanctuary for armed men.'

The request was made by the UN envoy Youssoufou Bamba before planned cuts to Ivory Coast's current 9,500 peacekeeping force to around 8,000 in July, with further reductions in 2015.

But there are ongoing concerns about the security situation in the country – the world's largest cocoa producer and once a major economic powerhouse for the West Africa sub-region.

'Ivory Coast still faces serious threats that need to be addressed to ensure lasting stability,' wrote the UN secretary general, Ban Ki-moon, in a recent report. 'Disarmament and reintegration of ex-combatants from both political camps, which remain crucial in resolving a serious threat against sustainable peace in the country, will be a challenge.'

Ivory Coast – whose previous violence has culminated around disputed elections – will go to the polls in 2015. The former president Laurent Gbagbo is currently being held at the international criminal court in The Hague where he has been charged with four counts of crimes against humanity, with further indictments against other senior Ivorian figures expected in the coming months.

'The peace process in Ivory Coast is still fragile, and this is a period of time with three elections that could be significant flashpoints – with Burkina Faso, Nigeria and Ivory Coast all going to the polls in 2015,' said Alex Vines, head of the Africa programme at Chatham House. 'Is this really the time to be significantly reducing UN peacekeeping operations?'

'Drones are only as good as the ability to act on the intelligence that they then obtain,' Vines added. 'Whether a drone monitoring the west of Ivory Coast will be effective without significant numbers of boots on the ground has to be questioned.'

The use of unmanned surveillance drones as part of peacekeeping operations is controversial. In January the security council in effect agreed to the deployment drones for the first time in the Democratic Republic of the Congo (DRC) after a nine-month insurgency by M23 rebels in the mineral-rich eastern DRC attracted renewed attention to the conflict in the country. The move in the DRC – which already has the world's biggest peacekeeping operation, with more than 17,000 troops – follows years of resistance to the proposal, which is still opposed by neighbouring Rwanda.

The UNOCI said it would be closely watching events in the DRC to assess the viability of using drones in Ivory Coast.

'We are looking at the experience of drones by the UN peacekeeping operation in DRC, to see the outcome and learn lessons from that,' said Van den Wildenberg.

The deployment of drones in Ivory Coast would be expected to concentrate on the troubled border area with Liberia, where there have been outbursts of fighting and civilian deaths in recent months, but where experts say the security situation is now improving.

Ivory Coast also shares poorly controlled borders with Guinea, which recently sent troops into the country in a dispute over border demarcations; Ghana, where a number of high-profile allies of Gbagbo have fled; and Mali, where an international military force is still fighting a war against al-Qaida-linked insurgents in the north.

17 April 2013

⇨ The above information is reprinted with kind permission from *The Guardian*. Please visit www.guardian.co.uk for further information.

Nuclear weapons: an 'evolving threat'?

By John Humphrys

John Humphrys asks: do the threats posed by Iran and North Korea gaining nuclear weapons mean that Britain too must remain a nuclear power?

Yet again talks aimed at preventing Iran from building its own nuclear weapons have broken down. Meanwhile, North Korea is rumoured to be about to undertake a fourth underground nuclear test to enhance its own nuclear capability just as its rhetoric against South Korea and the United States becomes more belligerent. David Cameron says all this shows that the threat posed to Britain by other countries gaining nuclear weapons means we too must remain a nuclear power. Is he right?

Catherine Ashton, the EU's high representative for foreign affairs, said after the failed talks with Iran this weekend that the two sides 'remain far apart on substance'. The negotiators – the five permanent members of the UN Security Council (the US, Russia, China, Britain and France) together with Germany – have been trying to persuade Iran to curtail its programme of enriching uranium. Iran says the programme is intended purely for civil nuclear energy purposes but few other countries believe them. They are convinced Iran wants to build its own nuclear weapons and that the enrichment programme is part of that plan.

In particular, Israel is certain this is what Iran intends to do and sees itself as in the immediate firing line, not least because Iranian leaders so often publicly state their belief that Israel has no right to exist. The combination of talks and economic sanctions has so far failed to pressure Iran into agreeing anything that satisfies those who are suspicious of its intentions.

Both Israel and the US have made clear that they are simply not willing to allow Iran to become a nuclear power. Not only do they think this would pose an intolerable threat to Israel (itself a nuclear power), but they believe it would set off a nuclear arms race in the Middle East. Saudi Arabia, Egypt and Turkey, among other countries, would then want their own nuclear weapons, it's believed.

So if talks fail, both Israel and the US have left open the option of using military means to thwart Iran's ambition. This could certainly delay Iran becoming a nuclear power; however, many commentators believe military action would not only exacerbate tensions in an already highly tense region but also serve to convince Iranian leaders that their ultimate security depended on achieving nuclear status.

North Korea is already much further down the road to being a nuclear state. It has built up a huge arsenal of missiles, some of which are thought to have an intercontinental range and some to be capable of carrying nuclear warheads. No one outside North Korea can be certain, however. What is clear is that North Korea has been holding underground nuclear tests, the third of which caused the United Nations to impose sanctions on the country last month.

It is in response to these sanctions that the North Korean regime has hit back with increasingly belligerent rhetoric. It has said it is now in a state of war with the South, has threatened to restart a nuclear reactor closed down after an earlier agreement, told foreign diplomats in Pyongyang that it can no longer assure their safety and threatened to use its nuclear weapons against both the South and the US.

In the case of both Iran and North Korea, however, domestic politics is widely believed to be playing as much a role in these recent increases in tension as anything else. In North Korea, sabre-rattling against the outside world is a familiar response to internal difficulties. In the current case it is being interpreted as a means to shore up the image of the young and newly-appointed leader, Kim Jong-un, in order to make him appear as resolute and defiant as his father and grandfather before him. William Hague, the Foreign Secretary, said over the weekend that it was important to stay calm in the face of provocations born of paranoia, though he added: 'We have to be concerned about the danger of miscalculation by the North Korean regime.'

With respect to Iran, some commentators see forthcoming presidential elections as the real reason for the country's refusal to come to an agreement.

It was in the context of these anxieties about other countries' nuclear ambitions that the Prime Minister addressed the issue of Britain's own future as a nuclear power when he visited the home of our nuclear submarines at Faslane in Scotland last week. He said bluntly that Britain needed a nuclear deterrent more than ever because uncertainty and risk had increased in the world.

Mr Cameron said: 'We need our nuclear deterrent as much today as we did when a previous British government embarked on it over six decades ago. Of course the world has changed dramatically. The Soviet Union no longer exists. But the nuclear threat has not gone away. In terms of uncertainty and potential risk it has, if anything, increased. Does anyone seriously argue that it would be wise for Britain faced with this evolving threat today, to surrender our deterrent? Only the retention of our independent deterrent makes clear to any adversary that the devastating cost of an attack on the United Kingdom or its allies will always be far greater than anything it might hope to gain.'

But, of course, not everyone in Britain agrees. Some have always been opposed to our having nuclear weapons as a matter of principle. They argue that the only point in having nuclear weapons is if the threat to use them is real, but they believe it is simply immoral to threaten innocent civilians in another country with nuclear annihilation.

Others, however, took a different view during the Cold War. They believed that the nuclear-armed Soviet Union posed a genuine threat to Western Europe, including Britain, and that the only way to contain that threat was for the West to have its own nuclear weapons as a deterrent against Soviet attack.

But many of those who took this view now look at the changed world in a different way from the Prime Minister. They argue that neither Iran nor North Korea (nor, for that matter, other recent nuclear powers like Israel, India and Pakistan) pose a remotely conceivable threat to Britain. Furthermore, they argue, whilst it may be alarming to contemplate countries run by unstable regimes having control of nuclear weapons, deterrence may no longer work in such cases. A madman really intent on using his country's nuclear weapons will not be deterred by our ability to retaliate, they say.

So increasing numbers of people who used to support Britain's nuclear deterrent are having second thoughts. And the need to come to a decision in the middle of this decade on whether or not to replace our existing Trident system is focusing minds.

David Cameron is committed to a like-for-like replacement that will cost tens of billions of pounds. The Liberal Democrats and Labour (and, indeed, some Tories) are wondering whether there might be a cheaper option, for example by no longer having one nuclear-armed submarine always permanently at sea, or by abandoning a submarine-based deterrent altogether in favour of a system using nuclear warheads on cruise missiles.

Others are asking whether we need a nuclear deterrent at all. Some are arguing that at a time when our conventional forces are being stretched to breaking point, as spending cuts fail to be matched by any reduction in the demands we make on those forces, scarce defence resources should be channelled into conventional forces even if that means we cease to be a nuclear power.

We are going to hear a lot more of this argument in the next few years. In the meantime we need to think about how threatened we feel (or not) by Iran and North Korea.

8 April 2012

⇨ The above information is reprinted with kind permission from YouGov. Please visit www.yougov.co.uk for further information.

Getting it right: the pieces that matter for the Arms Trade Treaty

An extract from the Oxfam Briefing Paper.

Arms and bullets continue to destroy lives. Every continent in the world is marred by devastation caused by armed violence. Yet there is still no effective international regulation of the global arms trade.

The need for an Arms Trade Treaty (ATT), which will create globally binding regulation of the international trade in conventional weapons for the first time, is greater than ever. Negotiators at the second and final Diplomatic Conference in March 2013 must deliver a treaty text that holds countries to the highest standards.

Summary

Arms and bullets continue to destroy lives. Every continent in the world is marred by devastation caused by armed violence – and it is ordinary people who are paying the ultimate price with more than one person dying per minute as a direct result of armed violence. Yet there is still no effective international regulation of the global arms trade.

Take for instance the ongoing violence in Syria. The UN has said that nearly 70,000 people have been killed and hundreds of thousands wounded since uprisings began in 2011. Much of this has been fuelled by arms transfers to both the Syrian Government and opposition forces.

The poorly controlled flow of weapons and ammunition around the world fuels the spiralling death toll. Gunrunners continue to operate with impunity on the shady fringes of this deadly trade. And, lax or non-existent reporting obligations make it almost impossible to tell in whose hands a gun, shell, bullet, or even fighter plane, will ultimately end up, or how it got there.

The need for an Arms Trade Treaty (ATT), which will create globally binding regulation of the international trade in conventional weapons for the first time, is greater than ever.

It has been eight months since the July 2012 Diplomatic Conference failed to reach agreement on an ATT. This month (March 2013), states will get a second chance. Time spent in July 2012 was not wasted; it did generate a draft treaty text, and then in October 2012, the UN General Assembly passed a resolution mandating a further negotiating conference. The resolution received unprecedented support: 157 votes in favour, 18 abstentions and no votes against, demonstrating clearly that the vast majority of member states want an ATT and providing them with a second chance to achieve that goal.

History shows that the most effective treaties are born from strong, comprehensive standards, established from the very outset. Treaties with weak provisions – no matter how broad their support – rarely become strong over time. Even where important countries do not sign, strong treaties have a positive influence on the actions of non-signatories. But some countries are prioritising universal agreement on the text and are willing to accept a draft treaty riddled with loopholes. If the ATT is really to make a difference in transforming the global arms trade, the second and final Diplomatic Conference must produce a treaty text that holds countries to the highest standards.

The text itself

The draft treaty that emerged from the July 2012 negotiations included some very positive elements. However, many of these could be undermined by a number of loopholes that considerably weaken the potential effectiveness of the ATT. In its current form, the treaty does not do enough to increase responsibility and restraint in international arms transfers, leaving millions of people at the mercy of irresponsible arms deals.

The scope of the treaty must include all types of conventional weapons, including ammunition,

and parts and components. It must regulate all types of arms transfers, including exports, gifts and loans.

There are inherent dangers with narrowly defining the scope of the treaty. As we have said before, a gun without bullets is a heavy metal stick. Therefore, it is essential ammunition is comprehensively covered. If all types of transfer are not included, there is a real risk that a variety of ways in which arms move across borders or change possession will be excluded from the ATT. This includes loans, leases, gifts and military aid. These weaknesses in the scope will prevent the treaty from having a meaningful impact on the lives and livelihoods of countless communities across the world.

The text of the ATT must introduce clear and strong rules governing the movement of arms and ammunition, with a clear obligation for states to refuse transfers where there is a substantial risk that those arms would be misused. The list of risks needs to be comprehensive, reflecting the humanitarian and human rights concerns that have driven the ATT initiative from the outset.

Compliance

To have teeth, the treaty must have strong compliance measures. It is vital that this part of the treaty is as watertight as possible, with realistic and achievable requirements. A worthwhile treaty will build on existing best practice, rather than undermining it. The loophole whereby arms transferred as part of a defence cooperation agreement would be exempt from the ATT, for example, threatens to undermine its entire object and purpose.

With numerous caveats and exemptions within the reporting obligations, the treaty as it stands would not lift the shroud of secrecy surrounding the global arms trade; while weak provisions for regulating the activities of arms brokers mean that the current treaty text would do little to rein in the unscrupulous middle-men who are so often at the centre of illicit and irresponsible international arms transfers.

		The SIPRI Top ten arms-producing and military services companies in the world, excluding China, 2010	
Rank 2010	Rank 2009	Company	Country
1	1	Lockheed Martin	USA
2	2	BAE Systems	UK
3	3	Boeing	USA
4	4	Northorp Grumman	USA
5	5	General Dynamics	USA
6	6	Raytheon	USA
S	S	BAE Systems Inc. (BAE Systems, UK)	USA
7	7	EADS	Trans-European
8	8	Finmeccanica	Italy
9	9	L-3 Communications	USA
10	10	United Technologies	USA

Note: an S denotes a subsidiary company.

Source: SIPRI.

While this represents a significant list of challenges, the March 2013 Diplomatic Conference does provide governments with the opportunity to achieve a robust and comprehensive ATT – one which will curb the irresponsible trade in arms, save lives and reduce the suffering of millions affected by the ravages of war and armed violence. States must ensure that the treaty text establishes high common international standards, while resisting pressures to water down provisions for the sake of universal support for the text.

Recommendations

The scope of the treaty must be fully comprehensive. It must control all types of conventional weapons, ammunition and munitions, and parts and components. It must also cover all the ways in which international arms transfers take place. The criteria of the treaty must be robust, and ensure that arms must not be transferred if there is a substantial risk that they would be used to commit serious violations of International Human Rights Law or International Humanitarian Law, exacerbate armed violence and conflict – including gender-based armed violence – encourage corruption or undermine development.

The implementation provisions must ensure that public reporting on all transfers is an obligation on member states, and that activities such as brokering are carefully and comprehensively covered.

The final provisions must ensure rapid entry-into-force of the treaty, and define amendment provisions that allow the States Parties to revisit the treaty over time.

12 March 2013

⇨ The material on pages 16 and 17, from *Getting it right: the final push to negotiate a strong Arms Trade Treaty* [http://policy-practice.oxfam.org.uk/publications/getting-it-right-the-pieces-that-matter-for-the-arms-trade-treaty-271706, 2013] is reproduced with the permission of Oxfam GB, Oxfam House, John Smith Drive, Cowley, Oxford OX4 2JY, UK. www.oxfam.org.uk Oxfam GB does not necessarily endorse any text or activities that accompany the materials.

© Oxfam 2013

Dynamics of internal displacement

There are currently nearly 25 million people uprooted within their own country by conflicts and human rights violations, a number that has remained stable for several years during which some IDP (internally displaced persons) situations have ended while others have begun or continued.

Regional overview of internal displacement

Africa is the region/continent worst affected with more than 13 million IDPs. Rebel activities and inter-communal violence were key factors in the displacement of civilians; although in several countries, government armies or proxy forces also forced people to flee. In Latin America, the bloody conflict in Colombia with its complex displacement patterns still accounted for nearly all new displacements. The region also continued to struggle to find durable solutions for people uprooted in conflicts that had long ended. In Peru and Guatemala, the return and reintegration of the displaced was agreed in the mid-1990s, but these agreements have never been fully implemented.

The Internal Displacement Monitoring Centre (IDMC) estimates that, by the end of 2004, some 3.3 million people were displaced within Asia-Pacific region due to conflicts. In addition come the approximately 1.2 million people displaced by the tsunami disaster in December 2004, and the large number of people displaced by development projects. From 4.6 million two years ago, the number of IDPs has decreased by nearly 30 per cent in the region. The intensification of ongoing conflicts opposing governments and rebel movements has been the main cause of new displacement during 2004.

In Europe, the number of internally displaced has decreased steadily during the last years, but there are still three million IDPs, most of them in Eastern Europe and the Balkans and the majority displaced for many years. In 2003, the Russian Federation (Chechnya) was the only country in Europe where people were still at risk of being forcibly displaced by ongoing fighting in 2003.

About half of the 2.1 million IDPs from the Middle East – in Israel, Syria and Lebanon – have been displaced for two decades or longer. The largest group of IDPs in this region live in Iraq. Conflict and instability continue to generate internal displacement in Iraq.

Source: Internal Displacement Monitoring Centre (IDMC) 2004, 2005a (http://www.internal-displacement.org)

Causes

Causes of conflict-induced displacement can be divided into root causes and proximate causes. Root causes are those which initiate a conflict and its displacement, although these can be hard to isolate as most of today's conflicts must be understood as self-perpetuating and their resulting displacement can be seen not only as an effect of the conflict but also eventually as a cause of its continuation.

There is a considerable body of knowledge about the root causes of displacement. We know for instance that very few internally displaced are uprooted by inter-state conflicts. Most conflicts causing internal displacement are a combination of internal fighting and direct foreign military intervention, most often linked to civil war (IDMC, 2005a). The causes are fuelled by deep structural problems, often rooted in acute racial, ethnic, religious and/or cultural cleavages as well as gross inequities within a country. During the Cold War, these differences, tensions, oppressions and repressions were often supported by the control mechanisms behind the two superpowers. The end of the Cold War removed these external interests and resulted in the intensification of many internal conflicts and related displacement flows (Deng, 2003).

There is surprisingly little systematic research on the proximate or immediate triggering causes of displacement and on how different causes converge to necessitate people to move. Such information is mainly garnered from personal accounts in ethnographic studies. An exception is the work of Birkeland (2003a,b), which concludes that displacement in the Angolan highland region of Huambo is triggered by the deterioration of land and restricted access to food and other necessities caused by war, rather than by the war itself. The study shows how analysis of the true complexity of displacement can result in a deeper understanding of proximate causes and potentially contribute to improved assistance and even an end to displacement.

Internal displacement and the international migration regime

The reasons why people forced to flee remain within the borders of their country are many and various. Safe travel all the way to a border may not be possible, or factors such as age, disability and health may impede their transit (Mooney, 2003a). Restrictions on travel and the right to seek asylum may also be imposed by external countries. These are among the many global issues that must be taken into account when exploring the nature of internal displacement.

The number of refugees in the world is currently lower than it has been in many years, but this does not mean that the number of forced migrants has declined. During the 1990s it was estimated that up to 12 million refugees had returned to their countries of origin (Koser and Black, 1999), but many returnee populations remained displaced within their country upon return. This was, for example, the case with the return of most Kurdish refugees to northern Iraq after the Gulf War (Dubernet, 2001).

During the 1990s, stricter immigration policies in the Western world, together with the growing scale of the refugee problem and the changing nature of the international and political order, encouraged a new approach for dealing with forced migration advocated by the United Nations High Commissioner for Refugees (UNHCR) (Ogata, 1995). This new approach emphasised preventive protection and focused less exclusively on the situation of refugees in countries of asylum and more systematically on the situation of vulnerable populations in countries of origin (Barutciski, 1996; Duffield, 1997; UNHCR, 1997). The preventive protection approach is thus more concerned with the root causes of forced migration and with preventing refugee flows by protecting and assisting people before they are forced to cross a border (Ogata 1993) in other words emphases on the right to leave and the right to seek and enjoy asylum have been replaced by the right to remain (Hyndman, 1999; Ogata, 1993). Many consider the establishment by US and European troops of safe havens for internally displaced Kurds in Iraq during the 1991 Gulf crisis as a turning point marking a new willingness among the international community to intervene on behalf of the internally displaced (Hyndman, 2000; Van Hear, 1993).

The right to remain has been a disputed policy, as it touches on sensitive political considerations – in particular the principle of sovereignty. The idea that outsiders should not intervene in the internal affairs of a country had been pivotal to the international communities approach to dealing with IDPs. In the post-Cold War period, formal sovereignty has been upheld, but has been reshaped to create the space for external involvement. This change in the way sovereignty is understood is based on the view that international involvement becomes essential and legitimate when a humanitarian crisis is caused by a governments failure to fulfil its responsibility to its citizens (Cohen and Deng, 1998a; Martin, 2000).

The right to remain strategy is also problematised by the fact that in situations of civil war, many internally displaced find themselves within the war zone, often in great danger and with little possibility of being reached by aid agencies. This situation has led some policy analysts to contend that the right to remain policy violates the right to leave one's country and to seek asylum as outlined in the UN Declaration of Human Rights (Hyndman 2003).

Websites

Internal Displacement Monitoring Centre (IDMC) http://www.internal-displacement.org/

UNHCR http://www.unhcr.org/

See more at: http://www.forcedmigration.org/research-resources/expert-guides/internal-displacement/dynamics-of-internal-displacement#sthash.yWoDWUP9.dpuf.

17 August 2011

⇨ The above information is reprinted with kind permission from Forced Migration Online. Please visit www.forcedmigration.org for further information and a complete list of references used in this text.

© Forced Migration Online 2013

Reaching displaced families with vital relief supplies in Syria

By Bastien Vigneau

A few days ago (16 February) I took part in a joint UN mission to Karameh, in Syria's north-western Idleb Province, to deliver much needed relief supplies to thousands of displaced people.

Through this first convoy, which started from Damascus and involved eight UN agencies, UNICEF delivered as a first batch family hygiene kits and special hygiene kits for babies. UNICEF is also sending other supplies, including children's clothes and school kits containing educational supplies. UN sister agencies provided materials including food, blankets and medical supplies.

Nearly 25,000 people – displaced from their homes by the on-going conflict in Syria – are estimated to be living in makeshift shelters in locations near the Turkish border, including Karameh, El Qah and Atmeh.

The situation I saw at Karameh is dire. The entire camp hosts around 4,500 people, made up of mostly women and children. I saw some children walking barefoot in the mud with nowhere for them to play safely, as the whole area is swamped due to heavy rains.

Although some aid has been delivered previously (mostly tents, food rations and mattresses), insecurity and the difficulty of access has limited what could be done. The needs are great and people lack even the most basic of supplies.

There are some tents that shelter displaced families and very few heaters, which quickly run out of fuel. Families lack the basics, including food, clean water, blankets, clothes and latrines. Women and children, who have lost everything, are enduring harsh living conditions, including cold temperatures.

This camp has only eight toilets, which is nowhere near enough to meet the needs of thousands of people. The lack of sanitation facilities and their poor condition are placing children, in particular, at extremely high risk of disease.

During the mission, I met 15-year-old Walid* who has been living at the camp with his parents and five siblings for two months. Walid is originally from rural Damascus, in Syria's south, from where he and his family fled due to heavy fighting. Walid's youngest brother was only eight days old at the time.

When they arrived in Idleb, the family initially took shelter with relatives. But because of fighting in the area, they had to move again, this time to Karameh camp. At first, the family had their own tent, but a few days ago, they were joined by another family of eight, also displaced because of fighting. Now 16 people are crammed into a single tent. Each has only one meal a day because they share what little food they have.

But Walid doesn't complain. He says he is happy that his close friend, who is also 15-years-old, has joined him at the camp. They are able to get some respite from the tough conditions by sharing memories of happier days, including their time spent together at school.

Walid tells me that he feels frustrated because he is no longer able to go to school: 'My desire is to go to school,' he says, 'but since this is not possible, I want to find a job to help my family with some income.'

Walid shares with me his hope of becoming a doctor so that he can save people's lives. He also wants to help his seven-year-old brother, who suffers from asthma, but lacks in medicine and other supplies to ease his condition.

Walid's friend tells me that he wants to go to school too, but when he gets older, he wants to defend his country. When peace returns he thinks about becoming a teacher, although he is still uncertain.

A second convoy to this area, which will depart from Damascus next week, will keep supplying vital supplies to the tens of thousands of people who desperately need help in this area of north-western Syria. I will again be part of the mission. While the security situation remains a key challenge, we are highly committed to reach out to children and families in need, wherever they are located.

Lack of funding remains a major issue for UNICEF's work in scaling up its humanitarian response in Syria. UNICEF is appealing for US$68 million to provide urgent humanitarian assistance in Syria for water and sanitation, health and nutrition, education and psychosocial support as part of a UN-wide appeal issued last December. So far, less than 20 per cent of that amount has been received.

*Name has been changed.

21 February 2013

⇨ The above information is reprinted with kind permission from UNICEF. Please visit www.childrenofsyria.info for further information.

Nadia's story: 'I nearly gave up my two sons'

Nadia,* 43, has come to the Ajlun branch of the Jordanian Red Crescent with her 16-year-old daughter Wade and her twin sons Ali and Omar, aged five. Ali and Omar are both severely disabled.

She says: 'We made our escape over the mountains, walking for five hours. I came with 17 members of my family. Many people came – there were 5,000 people at the same time making this journey.

'I had to give my sons sleeping pills to make the journey. I had been carrying them for four days when we made the journey, I had pain in both my arms. During the journey I nearly gave up my sons. I was so exhausted I wanted, just for a moment, to leave them behind. I had 14 children with me when I made this journey, one of them is my grandchild.'

Nadia says: 'We have been here in Ajlun for 18 days. We are paying rent of 120JD. The apartment is unfurnished; we have nothing, not even basic items, not even mattresses to put my boys on to sleep. There are 16 of us in two rooms and one corridor. When we lived in Syria each family had their own house, but now we are living together. My home was destroyed.

'I have seen people killed. There was bombing. My father died ten days ago. He was in Der'a and he refused to leave. We need food, diapers, we need mattresses. We don't even have pillows, or enough clothes to use to make pillows. We are very worried about the winter season.

'My 16-year-old daughter had to leave school to help me with her brothers – they need care all the time. My other daughter, she was in the third year of her four-year mathematics degree. She had to leave her course in Damascus, and now she is here with us. Not being able to continue her studies makes her very upset – she cries often. It is a very frustrating situation.'

The Jordanian Red Crescent is helping the family, bringing some clothing, items for the children and a full kit of household items for the family. This includes items like cooking pots and pans, the things that people often cannot bring when they flee.

* Name has been changed.

⇨ The above information is reprinted with kind permission from The British Red Cross. Please visit www.redcross.org.uk for further information.

Note: The British Red Cross is a neutral and impartial organisation. It does not engage in controversies of a political, racial, religious or ideological nature.

© The British Red Cross 2013

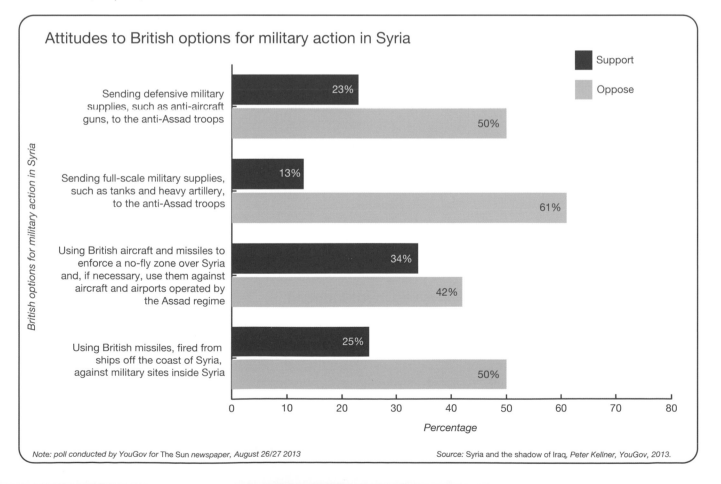

Attitudes to British options for military action in Syria

Note: poll conducted by YouGov for The Sun newspaper, August 26/27 2013

Source: Syria and the shadow of Iraq, Peter Kellner, YouGov, 2013.

What is forced migration?

Forced Migration Online (FMO) has adopted the definition of 'forced migration' promoted by the International Association for the Study of Forced Migration (IASFM) which describes it as 'a general term that refers to the movements of refugees and internally displaced people (those displaced by conflicts) as well as people displaced by natural or environmental disasters, chemical or nuclear disasters, famine or development projects'. FMO views forced migration as a complex, wide-ranging and pervasive set of phenomena. The study of forced migration is multidisciplinary, international and multisectoral, incorporating academic, practitioner, agency and local perspectives. FMO focuses on three separate, although sometimes simultaneous and inter-related, types of forced migration. These three types are categorised according to their causal factors: conflict, development policies and projects, and disasters.

These three categories of forced migration are often studied by different academic communities; the causes are addressed by different groups of policy-makers, donors and agencies; and the consequences addressed by different governmental, inter-governmental and non-governmental agencies, donors and organisations. FMO attempts to bring together in one place these various groups, approaches and experiences of all forms of forced migration.

Types of forced migration

1. Conflict-induced displacement

People who are forced to flee their homes for one or more of the following reasons and where the state authorities are unable or unwilling to protect them: armed conflict including civil war; generalised violence; and persecution on the grounds of nationality, race, religion, political opinion or social group.

A large proportion of these displaced people will flee across international borders in search of refuge. Some of them may seek asylum under international law, whereas others may prefer to remain anonymous, perhaps fearing that they may not be granted asylum and will be returned to the country from whence they fled. Since the end of the Cold War, there has been an escalation in the number of armed conflicts around the world. Many of these more recent conflicts have been internal conflicts based on national, ethnic or religious separatist struggles. There has been a large increase in the number of refugees during this period as displacement has increasingly become a strategic tactic often used by all sides in the conflict. Since the end of the Cold War there has also been an even more dramatic increase in the number of internally displaced persons (IDPs), who currently far outnumber the world's refugee population. In 2010, there were some 11 million refugees and asylum seekers and a further 27.5 million IDPs worldwide.

The most important international organisation with responsibility for refugees is the United Nations High Commissioner for Refugees (UNHCR). Under the 1951 UN Refugee Convention, UNHCR is mandated to provide protection and assistance to refugees. However, one group of refugees do not come under the mandate of UNHCR. These are Palestinian refugees in the Middle East, who come under the mandate of the United Nations Relief and Works Agency for Palestine Refugees in the Near East (UNRWA).

2. Development-induced displacement

These are people who are compelled to move as a result of policies and projects implemented to supposedly enhance 'development'. Examples of this include large-scale infrastructure projects such as dams, roads, ports, airports; urban clearance initiatives; mining and deforestation; and the introduction of conservation parks/reserves and biosphere projects.

Affected people usually remain within the borders of their home country. Although some are resettled, evidence clearly shows that very few of them are adequately compensated. While there are guidelines on restoration for affected populations produced by some major donors to these types of projects, such as the World Bank, there continues to be inadequate access to compensation. This tends to be the responsibility of host governments, and interventions from outside are often deemed inappropriate.

This is undoubtedly a causal factor in displacement more often than armed conflict, although it often takes place with little recognition, support or assistance from outside the affected population. It disproportionately affects indigenous and ethnic minorities, and the urban or rural poor. It has been estimated that during the 1990s, some 90 to 100 million people around the world were displaced as a result of infrastructural development projects. It has also been reported that, on average, ten million people a year are displaced by dam projects alone.

3. Disaster-induced displacement

This category includes people displaced as a result of natural disasters (floods, volcanoes, landslides, earthquakes), environmental change (deforestation, desertification, land degradation, global warming) and human-made disasters (industrial accidents, radioactivity). Clearly, there is a good deal of overlap between these different types of disaster-induced displacement. For example, the impact of floods and landslides can be greatly exacerbated by deforestation and agricultural activities.

Estimating trends and global figures on people displaced by

disaster is even more disputed and problematic than for the other two categories. But there are certainly many millions of people displaced by disasters every year. Several international organisations provide assistance to those affected by disasters, including the International Federation of the Red Cross and Red Crescent Societies, and the World Food Programme. Many NGOs (international and local) also provide assistance to affected people.

Types of forced migrants

There are various terms which have been adopted to describe groups affected by forced migration. The meaning of some of these terms is not always self-evident, they are sometimes misleading and are not necessarily mutually exclusive. Given below are brief descriptions of the main terms used by those researching and working with forced migrants.

Refugees

The term 'refugee' has a long history of usage to describe 'a person who has sought refuge' in broad and non-specific terms. However, there is also a legal definition of a refugee, which is enshrined in the 1951 United Nations Convention Relating to the Status of Refugees. Article one of the Convention defines a refugee as a person residing outside his or her country of nationality, who is unable or unwilling to return because of a 'well-founded fear of persecution on account of race, religion, nationality, membership in a political social group or political opinion'. Some 150 of the world's 200 or so states have undertaken to protect refugees and not return them to a country where they may be persecuted, by signing the 1951 Refugee Convention and/or its 1967 Protocol.

Those recognised as refugees are better off than other forced migrants, in that they have a clear legal status and are entitled to the protection of the UNHCR. The annual budget for the UNHCR has grown from US$300,000 in its first year to more than US$3.59 billion in 2012 and the agency works in 126 countries (UNHCR, 2012). The vast majority of refugees are in the world's poorest countries in Asia and Africa. The global refugee population grew from 2.4 million in 1975 to 14.9 million in 1990. A peak was reached following the end of the Cold War with 18.2 million in 1993. In 2010, there was estimated to be some 10.5 million refugees around the world (UNHCR, 2011).

Asylum seekers

Asylum seekers are people who have moved across an international border in search of protection under the 1951 Refugee Convention, but whose claim for refugee status has not yet been determined. Annual asylum claims in Western Europe, Australia, Canada and the USA combined rose from some 90,400 in 1983 to 323,050 in 1988 and then peaked at 828,645 in 1992. Applications fell sharply by the mid-1990s but began to steadily rise again towards the end of the decade. By the end of 2004, asylum applications made in these Western countries had again dropped significantly and in 2010 the total number of asylum applications in 44 industrialised countries was estimated at 358,800; the fourth lowest in the past ten years (UNHCR, 2011).

As the numbers of asylum seekers rose during the 1990s and beyond, there was increasing scepticism from some politicians and the media, particularly in Western states, about the credibility of the claims of many asylum seekers. They have been labelled 'economic refugees' and 'bogus asylum seekers'. Asylum migration is clearly a result of mixed motivations. Most asylum seekers do not come from the world's poorest states; however, many do come from failed or failing states enduring civil war and with high degrees of human rights abuses and, not surprisingly, significant levels of poverty. However, the number of people who are seeking asylum in Western states comprises a small fraction of the total number displaced around the world.

Internally displaced persons

The most widely used definition of internally displaced persons (IDPs) is one presented in a 1992 report of the Secretary-General of the United Nations, which identifies them as 'persons who have been forced to flee their homes suddenly or unexpectedly in large numbers, as a result of armed conflict, internal strife, systematic violations of human rights or natural or man-made disasters, and who are within the territory of their own country'.

Sometimes referred to as 'internal refugees', these people are in similar need of protection and assistance as refugees but do not have the same legal and institutional support as those who have managed to cross an international border. There is no specifically-mandated body to provide assistance to IDPs, as there is with refugees. Although they are guaranteed certain basic rights under international humanitarian law (the Geneva Conventions), ensuring these rights are secured is often the responsibility of authorities which were responsible for their displacement in the first place, or ones that are unable or unwilling to do so. The number of IDPs around the world is estimated to have risen from 1.2 million in 1982 to 14 million in 1986. However, it is likely that earlier estimates are woefully low, as little systematic counting was being conducted at the time. Estimates on numbers of IDPs continue to be controversial, due to debate over definitions, and to methodological and practical problems in counting. In 2010 there were an estimated 27.5 million IDPs worldwide (IDMC, 2011). However, statistics on IDPs are a controversial issue and there is no universal agreement.

27 January 2012

⇨ The above information is reprinted with kind permission from Forced Migration Online. Please visit www.forcedmigration.org for further information and a complete list of references used in this text.

© *Forced Migration Online 2013*

FAQs about child soldiers

Why do children join armed forces or armed groups?

Children join armed forces or groups for many reasons. In some situations children are forcibly recruited as a result of coercion, abduction or under threat of penalty. However, many children 'volunteer' often as a result of economic or social pressures, or because they believe the group will offer an income, food or security.

Children are particularly vulnerable to recruitment if they are poor, separated from their families, displaced from their homes, living in a combat zone or have limited access to education.

Is the child soldier problem worse among armed groups than government armed forces?

Child soldier use by non-state armed groups is widespread: dozens of groups are known to unlawfully recruit and use boys and girls. However, the record of some governments is also poor. Since 2010, child soldier use by 20 states has been reported either directly in government armed forces or indirectly in armed groups which they support or are allied to. In addition, around 40 states still have a minimum voluntary recruitment age below 18 years.

Child Soldiers International considers that any military recruitment of under-18s creates unnecessary and unacceptable risks to children.

Are there girl child soldiers?

Girls are recruited and used as soldiers in virtually all conflicts. They are most often present in non-state armed groups but are also used by government forces. Though exact numbers are impossible to know, worldwide estimates suggest that girls may account for between ten and 30 per cent of children in fighting forces. Girls are used to perform similar tasks to boys in both combat and non-combat roles. They are especially vulnerable to sexual violence.

There have been repeated calls to take into account the special needs and vulnerabilities of girls affected by armed conflict and to consider their requirements during disarmament, demobilisation and reintegration (DDR) process.

Should child soldiers who have committed war crimes or other serious violations of human rights or humanitarian law be held to account?

International human rights and child protection experts generally recognise that child soldiers are first and foremost victims of grave abuses of human rights, and that states must prioritise the prosecution of those who unlawfully recruit and use them.

Child soldiers should never be prosecuted solely for their association with the armed forces or group. However, there will be cases where a child soldier was clearly in control of his or her actions, was not coerced, drugged, or forced into committing atrocities. In such cases, excluding criminal responsibility for these children may deny justice to the victims and may also not be in the child's own best interests.

While in these cases criminal investigations and prosecutions should not be ruled out a priori, the individual concerned must be afforded all the guarantees and protection of international juvenile justice standards.

Where are child soldiers used today?

There have been reports of child soldier use in the following countries since January 2011:

Afghanistan: national army and other elements of state security forces; armed opposition groups.

Central African Republic: state-allied armed groups.

Colombia: national army (for intelligence purposes); armed opposition groups.

Côte d'Ivoire: national army/state security forces; state-allied armed groups; armed opposition groups.

Democratic Republic of the Congo: national army and other elements of state security forces; Congolese and foreign armed opposition groups.

India: armed opposition groups.

Iraq: elements of state security forces.

Israel: national army (for intelligence purposes).

Libya: national army and other elements of state security forces; armed opposition groups.

Mali: armed opposition groups.

Myanmar: national army and other elements of state security forces; armed opposition groups.

Pakistan: armed opposition groups.

Philippines: national army (for intelligence purposes) and other elements of state security forces; armed opposition groups.

Thailand: other elements of state security forces and armed opposition groups.

Somalia: national army; state-allied armed groups; armed opposition groups.

Sudan: national army and other elements of state security forces; state-allied armed groups; armed opposition groups.

South Sudan: national army; armed opposition groups.

Syria: national army and state-allied armed groups (use of children as human shields); armed opposition groups.

Yemen: national army and other elements of state security forces; state-allied armed groups; armed opposition groups.

⇨ The above information is reprinted with kind permission from Child Soldiers International. Please visit www. child-soldiers.org for further information.

© Child Soldiers International 2013

The children that will never grow old

The effects of war, the rise in food prices, hunger and climate change have prevented millions of children in the world from enjoying their childhood.

By Tatiana Martínez Hernández

According to the 2011 report by the United Nations Educational, Scientific and Cultural Organization (UNESCO), more than two million children were killed and another six million were permanently disabled in armed conflict between 1998 and 2008.

Foreign military intervention, civil war and extreme violence, which is often drug-related, halts the lives of those that have barely started it. There are numerous examples of this. In just 22 days, from 27th of December 2008 to 18th of January 2009, 350 children were killed and 1,815 were injured in the Israeli military attack on Gaza according to UN figures.

'Statistical sources for Chad and the Central African Republic say that nearly half of children under five-years-old living in warring regions suffer from rickets'

The US war and the North Atlantic Treaty Organisation's (NATO) 'crusade against terrorism' in Afghanistan in 2001 caused more civilian casualties, the majority of which were women and children, than all the military casualties of the intervening countries as a whole.

In 2009 alone, 1,000 children died in this central Asian territory due to bombings, combat between foreign forces, the government and insurgency, according to the UNESCO *Education for All* report in 2011.

This report states that between April and December 2009 the conflict in Iraq affected 223 children. Nevertheless, the analysis does not reflect the magnitude of damage caused by foreign troops that invaded and occupied Iraq from 1991 to 2003 and Afghanistan since 2001, not to mention the rising number of victims of the attacks in Libya.

Somalia, Pakistan, Sri Lanka, Sierra Leone, Democratic Republic of Congo (DRC), Bosnia and Herzegovina and Rwanda are examples of countries where conflict has caused a high number of deaths.

The DRC conflict (1998 to 2003) considered the most lethal since the Second World War, killed 5.4 million people.

Almost half were under five, which represented a fifth of the Congolese population.

These figures aren't sufficient in conveying the dangers that children must face in such situations and the consequences for future generations. An example of this is the Somali conflict where intermittent war has lasted more than 20 years and there are young people living their lives in the midst of combat.

UNESCO's 2010 report states that the number of child casualties does not adequately reflect the consequences that violence leaves behind such as the psychological trauma, the loss of their parents, siblings and friends.

'In just 22 days, from 27th of December 2008 to 18th of January 2009, 350 children were killed and 1,815 were injured in the Israeli military attack on Gaza according to UN figures'

NATO admitted in a statement that a recent bombing in the southern Afghan city of Helmand killed 12 children and two women due to confusion between the home of innocent civilians and trench insurgency. They sought forgiveness from family and friends of the victims.

Libya is currently experiencing a complex drama which should put the governments of the world on alert. Aicha, a young woman from Tripoli reported on rebeldia.org that missiles launched against her town by NATO are supposedly to protect civilians. But people walk freely along the road and children can play in the street.

United Nations agencies, NGOs and the global community have made repeated calls to end global violence and to respect the Geneva treaties concerning the protection of civilians living in areas of conflict.

Many of the military situations in recent years have occured in developing countries, where there are emergency situations of famine, severe droughts, floods and land slides, which causes a situation of humanitarian catastrophe, says the UN.

Statistical sources for Chad and the Central African Republic say that nearly half of children under five-years-old living in warring regions suffer from rickets. Around 195 million children aged one to five suffer from this disease, which causes stunted growth due to malnutrition and calcium deficiency, among other factors.

Famine and war

More than three million children die as a result of malnutrition and, although it is rarely cited as a direct cause of death among children, it is responsible for more than half of them, says the World Health Organization.

The illnesses associated with malnutrition and infection affect growth and development both biologically, psychologically and socially into adulthood.

Hence the need to ensure adequate support in the early years as recommended by experts.

However, the rising prices from the middle of last year of staple foods means that the problem of starvation among millions of infants will only get worse, particularly in poor countries.

According to a report by Oxfam, the cost of these products will more than double over the next 20 years, due in large part to the effects of climate change.

Those affected most will be the populations of poor countries, particularly in East Africa where more than eight million people, mostly women and children, suffer from severe food shortages.

The highest numbers of acute malnutrition are in the following countries: Djibouti, Ethiopia, Kenya and Somalia. The latter is one of the worst-affected countries in the world where one in four children suffers from extreme malnutrition.

Sub-Saharan Africa holds a fifth of the world's child population and records half of the number of deaths among young children on the planet and this figure is forecast to rise according to a report by the World Bank and International Monetary Fund.

Each year more than six million children die in the first 12 months of life, the majority of them in the month after birth. Pneumonia, diarrhoea, malaria and AIDS are the cause of one third of deaths among children under five years, many of which could be avoided, says UNESCO.

'Sub-Saharan Africa holds a fifth of the world's child population and records half of the number of deaths among young children on the planet'

It is proven that childhood is the happiest stage of a person's life when there are state directives in place for their care and protection.

In conclusion, we are witnessing the downfall of a planet with unsustainable lifestyles, which has the largest impact on vulnerable groups such as children, and in this sense Cuba is one of the few honourable exceptions.

3 July 2011

⇨ The above information was originally published by *The Prisma* and is reprinted with kind permission. Please visit www.theprisma.co.uk for further information.

© *The Prisma/Tatiana Martínez Hernández 2011*

Responsibility to Protect

What is the Responsibility to Protect?

The Responsibility to Protect (RtoP or R2P) is a new norm to prevent and stop genocide, war crimes, ethnic cleansing and crimes against humanity. The Responsibility to Protect is not a law, but rather a political commitment to guide states and sub-regional and international arrangements in protecting populations from these crimes and violations.

The Responsibility to Protect stipulates that:

⇨ The state bears the primary responsibility to protect its populations from genocide, war crimes, ethnic cleansing and crimes against humanity. This responsibility entails the prevention of such crimes and violations, including their incitement

⇨ The international community has a responsibility to assist and encourage the state in fulfilling its protection obligations

⇨ The international community has a responsibility to take appropriate diplomatic, humanitarian and other peaceful means to help protect populations from these crimes. The international community must also be prepared to take collective action, in a timely and decisive manner, in accordance with the UN Charter, on a case-by-case basis and in cooperation with relevant regional organisations, if a state fails to protect its populations or is in fact the perpetrator of crimes. Such action may entail coercive measures, including the collective use of force, where appropriate, through the UN Security Council.

Why is the Responsibility to Protect necessary?

The Holocaust and later genocides in Cambodia and Rwanda as well as crimes against humanity in the former Yugoslavia, East Timor and Darfur demonstrated massive failures by the international community to prevent atrocities. These cases of unconscionable suffering and the loss of millions of lives gave impetus to the call 'never again!'

Throughout the 1990s, controversy raged between those who supported a right to intervene to protect populations (i.e. humanitarian intervention) and those who argued that state sovereignty, as recognised by the UN Charter, precluded any intervention in internal matters. In Rwanda, the international community failed to take measures to protect populations from grave atrocity crimes; however, in the case of Kosovo, the North Atlantic Treaty Organisation (NATO) launched a military operation to end a humanitarian disaster without authorisation from the UN Security Council. These varied reactions, with civilians' lives at stake, illustrated the urgent need for an international consensus on when and how to take action to prevent and end mass atrocities, and led to a renewed understanding that the

security of the community and the individual, not only the state, must be urgent priorities for national and international policies. Recognising this, then UN Secretary-General Kofi Annan, in his addresses to the General Assembly in 1999 and 2000, challenged Member States to reconcile the principle of state-sovereignty and the responsibility of the international community to protect populations from massive human rights violations.

What are the four crimes and violations included in RtoP?

RtoP has a very narrow scope, and applies to only four specific crimes and violations: genocide, crimes against humanity, war crimes and ethnic cleansing. As such, the norm does not apply to other threats to human security including health crises, natural disasters, poverty or corruption. We often use the term 'mass atrocities' to encompass all four crimes and violations.

Genocide

After the horrors of the Holocaust, Member States in the UN General Assembly adopted the Convention on the Prevention and Punishment of the Crime of Genocide on 9 December 1948. Article II defines the term 'genocide' as:

Acts committed with intent to destroy, in whole or in part, a national, ethnical, racial or religious group, including:

⇨ Killing members of the group

⇨ Causing serious bodily or mental harm to members of the group

⇨ Deliberately inflicting on the group conditions of life calculated to bring about its physical destruction in whole or in part

⇨ Imposing measures intended to prevent births within the groups

⇨ Forcibly transferring children of the group to another group.

**Note: genocide can happen in or outside of armed conflict.

Crimes against humanity

The Rome Statute of the International Criminal Court was adopted on 1 July 2002 to establish the International Criminal Court, a permanent, international judicial body that can investigate and prosecute cases of genocide, crimes against humanity and war crimes. Not all governments are signatories to the Rome Statute, but Article VII of the Statute defines crimes against humanity (which unlike genocide, requires no specific intent) as:

Acts committed as part of a widespread or systematic attack directed against any civilian population, with knowledge of the attack:

⇨ Murder.

⇨ Extermination.

⇨ Enslavement.

⇨ Deportation or forcible transfer of population.

⇨ Imprisonment or other severe deprivation of physical liberty in violation of fundamental rules of international law.

⇨ Torture.

⇨ Rape, sexual slavery, enforced prostitution, forced pregnancy, enforced sterilisation, or any other form of sexual violence of comparable gravity.

⇨ Persecution against any identifiable group or collectively on political, racial, national, ethnic, cultural, religious, gender as defined in paragraph three, or other grounds that are universally recognised as impermissible under international law, in connection with any act referred to in this paragraph or any crime within the jurisdiction of the Court.

⇨ Enforced disappearance of persons.

⇨ The crime of apartheid.

⇨ Other inhumane acts of a similar character intentionally causing great suffering, or serious injury to body or to mental or physical health.

War crimes

On 12 August 1949, the international community adopted four Geneva Conventions. These and the two Additional Protocols, adopted in 1977, protect individuals who are not involved in hostilities during times of armed conflict. The Conventions and Additional Protocols articulate the standard of treatment for these individuals under international humanitarian law, and define a war crime as an act committed during an armed conflict that violates international humanitarian or human rights law. The range of violations that constitute war crimes is broad and, among others, includes murder or ill-treatment of anyone who is not or no longer taking part in hostilities, including civilians, prisoners of war, wounded or sick, medical and religious personnel and staff of relief operations.

**Note: war crimes under the Responsibility to Protect should be limited to crimes directed against civilian populations, committed in a widespread and systematic manner.

Ethnic cleansing

Ethnic cleansing is not officially recognised as a distinct crime under international law, but entails a purposeful policy designed by one ethnic or religious group to remove, by violent and terror-inspiring means, the civilian population of another ethnic or religious group from certain geographical areas. Thus, ethnic cleansing is encompassed in crimes against humanity, which includes the forcible transfer or deportation of populations.

October 2013

⇨ The above information is an extract from *A Toolkit on the Responsibility to Protect* and is reprinted with kind permission from the International Coalition for the Responsibility to Protect. Please visit www. responsibilitytoprotect.org to read the document in full, or for further information.

© *International Coalition for the Responsibility to Protect 2013*

When, if ever, is humanitarian intervention justified?

There are sometimes reckoned to be five criteria that, if achieved, mean humanitarian intervention is justified: these are similar to those set out by the ICISS Report in 2001 when dealing with the 'Responsibility to Protect' doctrine. The threat or harm carried out to the human population of the nation must be sufficiently clear and serious to justify the use of military force, so therefore there must be a seriousness of threat. The purpose of the intervention should be clear, so therefore it is important to know what threat is being dealt with, and that there are no other purposes or ulterior motives for the intervention. The humanitarian intervention, in order to be justified, must be used as a last resort.

Non-military options must be explored and there must be justification for having to resort to military action (which echoes international law on military force in general). Only if it is believed that lesser measures will not work then eventual military intervention is justified. The intervention should be done by proportional means and therefore

NOW... DO WE INTERVENE, OR NOT?

the scale of force, duration of action, and intensity of it so that it is the minimum necessary to deal with the threat in question. Most importantly to many scholars and in cohesion with the 'Just War' theory it must be clear that there is a reasonable chance that military action will be successful: by this it must be clear that the consequence of doing nothing, or rather, inaction, is greater than the consequence of intervention and action.

Since the end of the Cold War, there have been 13 cases of military humanitarian intervention, including the most recent incidents in Libya and Mali. The NATO mission in Yugoslavia (Kosovo) was considered a success, but the same procedures, except the 'boots on the ground', were used in the intervention within Afghanistan and there is little argument that the intervention within Afghanistan was in the slightest way successful.

Much the same argument goes with official UN missions. There was success in Libya, although in East Timor success was limited, and in the Democratic Republic of Congo the war has lasted 25 years and more lives have been claimed than in any war since World War Two. Furthermore, the lack of action by the UN in Rwanda in 1994, and more recently in Darfur, have been heavily criticised.

In terms of non-violent intervention, there is the same controversy but on a more subtle level. The Bill Gates Foundation donated $1.3 billion in 2012 to fight AIDS, tuberculosis and malaria amongst other things. If this donation in fighting these diseases in Africa is

a success then there is no doubt his humanitarian intervention will be described as justified and successful. Yet on the other hand, if the results provide nothing and the benefits are not seen, people will be questioning how much better off the $1.3 billion would have been spent elsewhere.

At the same time there are organisations such as the Catholic Church. Catholic Relief Services, representing the Church within the USA, distribute funds throughout the world for humanitarian causes. Many of these causes it funds are undoubtedly a success, and therefore justified, with their response to the Haiti Earthquake in 2010 being one of those. There has been controversy across Africa and South America in their campaign against the use of condoms, instead they fight for abstinence. In fighting against condoms, even though the message is pro-abstinence they still fight against the general spread of condoms at the same time, therefore damaging the campaign for the prevention of the spread of AIDS. This is because condoms are seen as the true devil here, as the message is twisted and abstinence is not adhered.

The UN meanwhile does great work around the world providing humanitarian relief: an example is managing displaced Palestinian refugees or providing earthquake relief, all being justified and often successful. Yet in October 2010, a hurricane hit Haiti before going on to the East Coast of the USA. Along with it came the death of 54 people in Haiti and tens of thousands of people left homeless: the UN sent relief workers from South Asia and they brought with them cholera – a disease Haiti had not seen in over a century. Since then more than 500,000 people have been infected by this disease with the death toll by the end of December 2011 being 7,000 deaths – more than the earthquake caused in the first place. This is an example of humanitarian intervention that is non-violent being far from being executed properly. Yet, had it been a success and thereby executed properly, it would have been justified. As is evident from here with both violent and non-violent cases there is no simple criteria that can judge justification, it is rather the success after that will measure whether it is considered justified or not.

In conclusion, as was proven from the onset, humanitarian intervention when executed properly is justified. It is only justified, though, when the criteria are met and if it is humanitarian in nature. In reality though, only afterwards can it be seen whether the intervention was justified, due to it depending mainly on success.

There were five criteria that were set up that would justify intervention. The threat being serious enough, a clear purpose of the reason for intervention, military action only as a last resort, intervention must be the minimum necessary and there must be a reasonable chance of success. All of these criteria lead to intervention being justified from the onset. Afterwards though, it will only be considered justified if the intervention was successful. If it is not successful, then it will not be considered justified. For this reason humanitarian intervention although justified, and justified when reaching the five criteria that were made clear, it is only in reality justified if the intervention was successful.

3 May 2013

⇨ The above information is reprinted with kind permission from The Backbencher. Please visit www.thebackbencher. co.uk for further information.

Yes, the UN has a duty to intervene. But when, where and how?

As Britain pushes for more intervention in Syria, a debate rages over if it is acceptable to use force in international relations.

By Peter Beaumont

The Russian foreign minister Sergei Lavrov, in a recent interview, produced a piece of paper from his pocket with a quote from Alexander Gorchakov, a 19th-century Russian prince who served as the tsar's foreign minister.

'Foreign intervention into domestic matters,' intoned Lavrov to Susan Glasser, Foreign Policy's editor-in-chief, 'is unacceptable. It is unacceptable to use force in international relations, especially by the countries who consider themselves leaders of civilisation.'

As ministers in the US, UK and France push for greater intervention to prevent Syria's bloodshed, Lavrov's remark stands not only as a rebuke to the ambitions of those who would do more to stop Bashar al-Assad, but to an entire doctrine of humanitarian intervention – Responsibility to Protect (R2P) – whose future is uncertain.

Drawn up by the UN in response to the wars of the 1990s, not least in Bosnia and Rwanda, which both saw atrocities that would be defined as genocidal, R2P was adopted by the UN as a 'norm' for dealing with conflicts where civilians were under attack in 2005.

Its language has been referred to – or invoked directly – to justify the French interventions in Ivory Coast in 2011, in Mali earlier this year, and the NATO-led no-fly zone imposed over Libya during the conflict that led to the fall of the Gaddafi regime. But now, facing precisely the kind of terrible conflict the doctrine was designed to mitigate or largely prevent, the brave new UN model for protecting civilian victims of war has stalled.

As both the US and the UK's defence secretaries indicated last week that they are examining different military options, a debate has erupted over the future of military interventions on humanitarian grounds, and their claimed necessity.

Those arguments have ranged from the moral to the utilitarian and the self-interested – witness the argument that by not acting the US, in particular, damages its future 'credibility' when it threatens the use of force. They have been made amid a rethinking of how these military interventions are actually conducted, from the large-scale operations and expensive, flawed, nation-building efforts that were seen in Iraq and Afghanistan to 'lighter footprint' interventions seen recently in Libya, Mali and Ivory Coast.

Opponents of different kinds of intervention in Syria have cited complex practical problems, including how to arm a rebel side numbering a significant minority of jihadist fighters. But one of the biggest stumbling blocks has been how R2P itself has been applied in the recent past – not least in Libya.

Gareth Evans, Australia's former foreign minister, is also an international lawyer jointly responsible for drafting the document taken on by the UN in 2005. He is among those who admit that a doctrine designed to give meaning to the promises of 'never again' made after the Holocaust and the killing fields of Cambodia, Bosnia and Rwanda has met difficulties. 'What punctured the optimism that the world might be on its way to ending internal mass atrocity crimes once and for all,' said Evans, 'is the controversy that erupted in the security council in 2011 about the way the norm was applied in the NATO-led intervention in Libya, and the paralysis that in turn generated in the council's response to Syria.' Last year Evans spoke of a collapse of international consensus that had led to 'paralysis' over Syria.

'I believe that – like most midlife crises – this one will prove survivable ... but I can't pretend that its full realisation will not be a work in progress for a long time to come.'

The deliberations over Libya, Evans argues, marked the 'high water mark' of R2P – seeing the new norm referred to in two UN security council resolutions authorising 'all necessary means' in the conflict. But the subsequent 'backlash' is still being felt today.

'The concern was about what came after when it became rapidly apparent [to Brazil, Russia, India, China and South Africa] that the three permanent council-member states driving the intervention [the US, UK and France, or 'P3'] would settle for nothing less than regime change, and do whatever it took to achieve that.

'Particular concerns were that the interveners rejected ceasefire offers that may have been serious, struck fleeing personnel that posed no immediate risk to civilians and locations that had no obvious military significance [like the compound in which Gaddafi relatives were killed] and, more generally, supported the rebel side in what rapidly became a civil war, ignoring the very explicit arms embargo in the process.'

For Russia, Libya provided confirmation of its objections to R2P in the first place. For other countries such as South Africa, which had backed the principle of a new norm for intervention to prevent atrocities, the use of R2P for regime change in Libya – and the refusal of the P3 to report on the progress of the operation and its new parameters – were seen as betrayal.

Jennifer Walsh, professor of international relations at Oxford University who has studied the development of R2P, agrees with Evans's analysis. But she also

identifies a 'moral hazard' inherent in R2P – that it can create a perception in conflicts that a rebel force may be only a regime-sponsored atrocity away from international interveners coming to its aid. The incentive for rebels to find a negotiated solution is thus reduced.

As Walsh points out, the suspicion that recent interventions have been too easily dominated by the agenda of the US, Britain and France has led to a push-back, led by Brazil.

The Brazilians and others are seeking to insist that any future military interventions on humanitarian grounds authorised by the UN should be guided both by a 'prudential' assessment of the practicality of achieving the desired outcome in complex conflicts and informed by a mechanism for transparent, real-time reporting of the progress of operations to council members, to prevent resolutions being used as blank cheques by the P3 countries.

This leaves the question of what the international community could do if it were proved definitively that chemical weapons had been used by the Assad regime in Syria, evidence that the British and US Governments were backing away from last week.

Some US officials in private have suggested that at best any change in policy would see the provision of small arms to the 'right rebels' in groups not tainted by association with jihadist elements, an even lighter footprint than the intervention in Libya. Others, including senators – such as John McCain – and analysts, have been calling for full-blown intervention. Options that have been mooted range from air strikes, to no-fly zones, the creation of safe havens and humanitarian corridors, and even a Bosnian-style soft partition of the country.

The Lib Dem peer, Paddy Ashdown, who was a soldier in Northern Ireland and then high representative in Bosnia after the war there, disagrees that Libya set a damaging precedent, but adds it would be 'folly' to intervene in Syria or lift the EU arms embargo.

'R2P was in some respects a way of legitimising the intervention in Kosovo.

I thought it would remain an aspiration but the effect of Libya was to turn from being a collection of words into being a precedent. It remains, however, a principle subject to the will of the powerful to enforce it.'

Ashdown believes, too, that the more limited intervention in Libya – despite the country's post-Gaddafi unrest and political instability – remains a far better model than the occupation of Iraq, leaving Libyans in charge of their own destiny.

'It was not perfect but it was far less of a mess than Iraq.'

Nonetheless, he argues forcefully that, even with the existence of R2P, a key test for intervention is whether it is both practically applicable or whether it will do more harm than good.

'One of the key lessons of interventions is the unintended consequences that follow,' he adds. Ashdown warns: 'There has been a tendency to see Syria in simplistic black and white – powerless civilians against a brutal dictator – without trying to understand the wider regional tension involved.'

Echoing Ashdown last week was Daniel C. Kurtzer, a former US ambassador to Egypt and to Israel, writing in *The New York Times*.

'Before making a momentous decision on intervention – especially if the president is considering unilateral intervention – we ought to first do serious diplomacy to see whether an international consensus can be reached on the question of intervention ...

'Indeed, the Syria crisis presents an opportunity to turn away from unilateralism and to adopt instead a more strategic, multilateral approach to resolving international crises.'

4 May 2013

⇨ The above information is reprinted with kind permission from *The Guardian*. Please visit www.guardian.co.uk for further information.

Establishing stability in Afghanistan

Issue

We are in Afghanistan for one overriding reason – to protect our national security by helping the Afghans take control of their own. We are helping Afghanistan develop the ability to maintain its own security and prevent the return of international terrorists, such as al-Qaeda.

To achieve this, Afghanistan is supported by a range of international partners to develop its security, governance, infrastructure, economy and ability to provide essential services.

Actions

Afghanistan is a top UK foreign policy priority and it is our defence main effort. We are one of more than 60 countries helping the Afghan Government establish the conditions to be able to protect its citizens, provide for their basic needs and determine the country's future, eventually without significant help from the international community. The British Embassy in the capital Kabul provides a focus for the UK's work in Afghanistan.

Military support

UN Mandate as part of NATO's International Security Assistance Force (ISAF).

The UK's military activities in Afghanistan are conducted under a UN Mandate as part of NATO's International Security Assistance Force (ISAF).

We are the second largest contributor to this coalition of 49 nations and the majority of our armed forces in Afghanistan operate in the southern province of Helmand. ISAF operates in support of the Afghan National Security Forces (ANSF) providing training, advice and some assistance to the Afghan Army and Police. The ANSF's ability to protect the population, provide a basic civilian policing service and prevent international terrorists from finding a safe haven in Afghanistan will all be crucial to Afghanistan's long-term stability. ISAF's practical support to the ANSF is now only for the more specialist capabilities such as surveillance, medical and air.

The transfer of responsibility for security to Afghanistan by 2014

The shared aim of President Karzai and the members of ISAF is that the transfer of responsibility for security to the ANSF is completed across the whole country by the end of 2014, when the ISAF mission is due to end.

The Afghans took a significant step forward to achieving that aim in June 2013 when the ANSF assumed lead responsibility for security across the whole of Afghanistan. The nature and size of the UK's presence in Afghanistan is changing. President Karzai and ISAF members have agreed to this process of change – known as 'Transition' – whereby full responsibility for security and governance is taken on by the Afghans. Transition is now in effect across the whole of Afghanistan.

The ANSF, established in 2002, is made up of the Afghan National Army (ANA), the Afghan Air Force (AAF) and the Afghan National Police (ANP). These forces are mentored and trained by ISAF forces and other specialists from the international community, for example British Police Officers.

ANSF units are growing in size and capability. They are approaching their maximum size of approximately 352,000. As their size and capability grows they are increasingly setting their own priorities, doing their own planning, leading operations and carrying out more specialist tasks such as dealing with roadside bombs, without the need for significant ISAF involvement.

In 2015 NATO will start a new, and smaller, non-combat mission in Afghanistan based on training, assisting and advising the ANSF. This will be known as RESOLUTE SUPPORT. This will take place alongside international community activities that will continue to support Afghanistan in non-security sectors.

UK support for Afghanistan's long-term development beyond 2014 was confirmed in the Enduring Strategic Partnership agreement signed by the Prime Minister and President Karzai of Afghanistan in January 2012. It reaffirmed both countries' commitment to a continuing partnership and friendship.

As part of the agreements made at the Chicago Summit in May 2012 the UK will contribute £70 million per year from 2015 to at least 2017 towards sustaining the ANSF. Our Armed Forces will also take the coalition lead in supporting a new Afghan National Army Officer Academy, which will help develop the next generation of Afghan military commanders.

Economic and social projects

We are helping Afghanistan to become a more viable state that can increasingly meet its population's needs from its own resources. This work includes support for economic and social development and helping the Afghan Government implement its National Drug Control Strategy.

The UK agreed to maintain our development assistance of £178 million a year until 2017 at the Tokyo Conference in July 2012. This support will help the Afghan Government to reduce extreme poverty, create jobs and achieve long-term economic growth.

The UK's development assistance is led by the Department for International Development. It concentrates on three main areas to increase stability and reduce poverty:

⇨ improving security and political stability

⇨ stimulating the economy

⇨ helping the Afghan Government deliver basic services.

The Stabilisation Unit deploys civilian experts such as police officers, prison governors, barristers and governance experts to Afghanistan to help the Afghan Government and its people in these three main areas.

Afghanistan's development into a more viable state is a long-term task that will continue to face many challenges. Our efforts are not designed to create a perfect Afghanistan but one that is able to maintain its own security and prevent the return of international terrorists.

The Provincial Reconstruction Team

The Provincial Reconstruction Team (PRT) is a UK-led, multinational effort of the UK, US and Danish Governments. It works with ISAF's Regional Command South West, helping the Afghan Government establish improved governance and development across Helmand Province.

As agreed by President Karzai and the international community, all PRTs across Afghanistan will close by the end of 2014, in keeping with developing Afghan sovereignty and transition. This includes Helmand.

During the remainder of its presence in Helmand, the PRT will focus on supporting the Government of Afghanistan reach inclusive political settlements backed by good governance, strong rule of law and sustainable development in line with the Government of Afghanistan's national ministry strategies, standards and priorities.

Background

The UK is in Afghanistan because the country had become a base for terrorists that threatened our country and the rest of the world. The Taliban government gave al-Qaeda safe haven in Afghanistan and this allowed terrorists to plan and carry out attacks around the world, most notably the 9/11 atrocities in 2001.

The Taliban were given the opportunity to help bring the leaders of al-Qaeda to account. When they refused to do so, action was taken by members of the international community to remove them from control of Afghanistan.

The al-Qaeda training camps and Taliban regime that provided them safe haven were dismantled in the months after 9/11.

Political settlement

The stability of Afghanistan will not be achieved by security activities alone and we are supporting Afghan efforts to achieve a political settlement that will secure peace and stability. The Prime Minister, Foreign Secretary and others are actively involved in trilateral talks with their Afghan and Pakistani counterparts. Everyone is committed to this and we have all called on the Taliban to break from al-Qaeda and participate in a peace process.

Case studies

Demining Herat: making land safe in Afghanistan's 'bread basket'

How UK aid and the HALO Trust are helping farmers reclaim their fields in Afghanistan.

Bost Agri-Business Park – a beacon for business potential

An innovative new business park will unlock the immense business potential of Helmand Province in Afghanistan, creating hundreds of new jobs and safeguarding existing ones.

Growing poppies instead of opium in Afghanistan

How improved security and agricultural support from the UK is helping Afghan farmers to move away from growing poppies to more sustainable crops.

Building furniture and a future in Afghanistan

How UK aid is helping small businesses succeed and grow.

28 February 2013

⇨ The above information is reprinted with kind permission from the Foreign & Commonwealth office. Please visit www.gov.uk for further information.

© Crown copyright 2013

Did the wars liberate Afghan and Iraqi women?

During the first few years after the US-led invasion, Iraqi women were used as yardsticks to show the progress the country was making towards democratisation and protection of human rights. However, coalition forces soon turned their attention from human security to national security. Iraqi women today have very little political influence and power to participate in decision-making. They also experience gender violence and poverty as a result of deteriorating infrastructure, the death, disappearance and detention of male spouses, and more conservative laws and attitudes than those in place ten years ago. These problems are exacerbated in a context of lack of rule of law and Prime Minister al-Maliki's systemic sidelining of political opposition.

Iraq's poor infrastructure and continuing humanitarian crisis impact the majority of Iraqi women's lives. Following the US-led invasion, the number of Iraqi women reduced to impoverished widowhood and refugee status skyrocketed. Poverty and insecurity, while widespread, are particularly apparent among women and men who are refugees, as well as women heads of households. Political will in Iraq to address the needs of these vulnerable populations is lacking. Minister of State for Women's Affairs Ibtihal Al-Zaidi stated in 2011 that the ministry 'has no jurisdiction over the directorate of women's welfare or increasing funds allocated to widows' and is 'no more than an executive-consultation bureau with a limited budget and no jurisdiction on implementing resolutions or activities'.

Iraqi women activists mobilize in the face of these political and economic setbacks. Since the 1920s, Iraqi women have pressed for access to legal rights, schooling and paid employment with notable success. While Iraqi women's organisations won a 25 per cent quota for women in the new legislature, the newly emerged political parties are all led by men and there is only one woman among the 44 members of the current cabinet – down from six female-headed ministries from 2005–2006. Iraqi women activists today express alarm at the country's gender policies, laws and politics, saying that the US Government's focus on reconciling Shiite, Sunni and Kurdish men's rivalries constantly marginalize important women's issues, such as access to education, health care, legal protection and paid employment. They have also been mobilizing against domestic violence, trafficking, and honour-based crimes, providing shelters and advice to victims

At a meeting among women's rights activists to launch Iraq's first-ever CEDAW (Convention on the Elimination of All Forms of Discrimination against Women), participants agreed that the rights and status of women have not been adequately considered by any of the political actors – international or Iraqi – involved in Iraq's post-conflict reconstruction and political transition. This is a telling reflection of how far the coalition forces have strayed from their original claim that the Iraq war would improve Iraqi women's lives.

The US-led war in Afghanistan followed on the heels of a war in the 1980s with the Soviet Union, and a 1990s civil war. Each war has turned thousands of Afghan women into refugees and widows – or both – and made it dangerous for women to seek schooling, healthcare, paid employment and legal rights. In each war, rival male combatants have claimed that they knew what was best for Afghan women, while marginalising women in the actual planning of their future. And in each war, women and their children were often the victims of the violence itself.

In its 2001 invasion of Afghanistan, the US Government chose as its chief domestic allies those warlords – the 'Northern Alliance' – opposed to Taliban rule. This was despite the fact that they firmly embraced negative or dismissive views of women, for instance, accepting domestic violence as a husband's prerogative. Currently, women hold a quarter of the seats in the Afghan legislature, but that percentage was gained over the objections of quota-phobic American officials. In addition, the millions of foreign dollars that have poured in for contractors and infrastructure have mainly benefited men and in many cases have created incentives for escalating conflict between male-led groups. Afghan women activists fear that the status of women – especially as it is affected by laws regarding marriage, inheritance, custody, divorce and domestic violence – will become mere bargaining chips among the rival foreign and local male elites.

Updated February 2013

⇨ The above article is kindly made available by the Costs of War Project, based at the Watson Institute for International Studies at Brown University. This article appears alongside other online resources, which can be found at www.costsofwar.org.

The papers posted alongside this article are:

What War Has Wrought in Afghan Women's Lives (Jennifer Heath), http://costsofwar.org/sites/default/files/AlAliPrattgender.pdf, (2011), accessed 25 October 2013. Originally published in a joint volume with Ashraf Zahedi, *Land of the Unconquerable: The Lives of Contemporary Afghan Women* (University of California Press, 2011).

Conspiracy of Near Silence: Violence Against Iraqi Women (Nadje Al-Ali & Nicola Pratt), (2011), http://costsofwar.org/sites/default/files/AlAliPrattgender.pdf, accessed 25 October 2013. Originally published in *Middle East Report*.

The Forgotten Story: Women and Gender Relations 10 Years After (Nadje Al-Ali), (2013), http://costsofwar.org/sites/default/files/Women_and_Gender1.pdf, accessed 25 October 2013.

Syria is not Iraq (but at least the Iraq War had a clear objective)

By Alex Massie

A decade ago, I was sure that going to war in Iraq was the right thing to do. I persisted in that belief for a long time too, well beyond the point at which most supporters of the decision to remove Saddam Hussein from power had recanted their past enthusiasm.

The link between 9/11 and Iraq was quite apparent. Not because (despite what some mistaken people insisted) Saddam had any involvement in the atrocity but because removing tyrants and dictators seemed the best way of spreading the pacifying forces of commerce and democracy that might, in time, render Islamist extremism and terrorism obsolete.

Why Iraq? Because it was there and because it could be done. Besides, there was unfinished business. Not just from 1991 but from 1998 and Operation Desert Fox as well. And, also, because it seemed obvious that sanctions were not working, that the sanctions regime would collapse and that Saddam would soon, if nothing was done, escape the 'box' in which he was said to be confined. And who knew what would happen then? Inaction has consequences too.

There were other arguments as well. I was at the United Nations to see Colin Powell's presentation on Iraq's weapons programmes. Powell made a powerful case that something had to be done to challenge Saddam. I wasn't alone in thinking that; diplomats from many countries, including plenty from nations with no immediate stake in the conflict, agreed.

A decade later that all seems hopelessly optimistic. Worse than that, naive. Nevertheless, that was where we were and what I believed. The arguments in favour of doing something were strong and compelling. Millions of people agreed, some reluctantly, others enthusiastically.

And there was something else too, something which gave the argument greater urgency: this was to be the great cause of our time, the great project that justified the expenditure of blood and gold in pursuit of a noble, historic, objective. This would be the anti-piracy or anti-slavery movement of our time.

So it has been a chastening decade. It did not work out like that and all that youthful certainty seems like reckless hubris now. But there is no point or advantage in denying how it seemed at the time.

It helped – and this is a point of which I am not especially proud – that so many of the wrong people were opposed to the war. Who wanted to be on the same side as George Galloway, Stop the War [sic] and Seumas Milne and all the rest of them?

We know a little better now. We have a better understanding of how little we can do and a more sensible appreciation of what we can realistically hope to achieve.

So it is hard – perhaps impossible – to contemplate the prospect of bombing Syria in isolation. Syria is not Iraq but the ghosts of Operation Iraqi Freedom can't be banished so easily. Refighting the last war is a foolish exercise but refusing to consider lessons from the past is folly too.

So, like Tom Harris, I would envy some people their certainty if I did not also suspect that certainty was misplaced. I agree with Chris Dillow's suggestion that: 'The fact that everyone seems to have an opinion on Syria tells us more about the ease [with] which opinions are formed that is does about what is actually happening in Syria.'

And it seems to me that the idealistic argument for intervention in Iraq a decade ago was stronger than the case for intervening in Syria today.

(That said case was subsequently shot to pieces by events is a different matter.) At least Iraq had a clear objective: removing Saddam Hussein from power. (Tony Blair would have avoided some difficulties if he had been clearer on that point.) Syria is different.

What, exactly, are we attempting to achieve? We are clear that we do not wish to remove Bashar al-Assad from power. So we do not think his use of chemical weapons is that big a deal. Certainly not a big enough deal to make the case for regime change.

The plan, in as much as there is one, seems to be to put him in detention rather than expel him. But to what end? Will bombing Syria persuade Assad to modify his behaviour? Is our objective to make him offer the rebels a 'fairer fight'? There are other questions too.

We do not want Assad to win but we do not want him to lose either. We certainly do not want to find ourselves in a position in which we are responsible for 'fixing' Syria in the future. That's realpolitik of the driest, coldest kind.

But once you bomb you are part of the conflict. How, having intervened once, can the United States and its allies walk away? Shoving Assad onto the naughty step seems an insufficient response to his misdeeds. If the aim is simply to persuade Assad that any further use of chemical weapons will bring additional consequences it might be wise to consider what those consequences might be.

In other words, what if spanking Assad does not work? How far are we prepared to go? What do we do next? And, for that matter, what great difference does it make to the Syrian people if they are killed by chemical weapons or by 'conventional' arms? Upon what grounds do we make that moral distinction ourselves? Chemical weapons are horrifying; so is war. Is it worse for 1,000 Syrians to be killed by chemical weapons than it is for 5,000 to be slaughtered by 'traditional' means?

I don't know. I know that the argument for doing something can seem preferable to doing nothing at all. But, again, what are we really hoping to achieve? Would a limited two day bombing campaign really provide the kind of exemplary punishment that would make other tyrants think twice before they wage war against their own citizens? Perhaps it would but that does not seem obvious either.

So for whom – and what – would we be fighting? Not for the Syrian opposition since, again, we do not really want them to win either. And not for the Syrian people either.

Not unless the objective is to inflict such damage upon Assad that he cannot win the war either and has no choice but to be dragged to a peace conference. But bringing Assad to heel most probably – surely – means accepting that he and his party must have a role and a place at any peace talks. Otherwise what, however much this sticks in the craw, is in it for him?

I'd like to share Michael Weiss's confidence that 'Conditions are fertile for the weakening of the jihadists at the expense of the moderates.' But even if this is so it suggests that even if Assad is defeated and eventually removed from power the United States and its allies will be returning to Syria to take sides in a second civil war between the jihadists and the (relative) moderates. Are we prepared for that too?

The current situation in Syria may be untenable; unfortunately that does not mean any of the plausible alternative scenarios are any more tenable. Or welcome. There is certainly a moral case for action and I do not think those who favour it should be dismissed as warmongering know-nothings. But the arguments against intervention are just as compelling.

Which means I do not know what David Cameron, Barack Obama, Francois Hollande and their arabian allies should do but I am suspicious of the certainty with which so many other people – on all sides of the discussion – seem to view this dilemma.

28 August 2013

⇨ The above information is reprinted with kind permission from *The Spectator*. Please visit www.spectator.co.uk for further information.

A more peaceful world awaits

Statistical analyses show that the world will be more peaceful in the future. In about 40 years only half as many countries will be in conflict. The decrease will be greatest in the Middle East.

By Yngve Vogt

In 1992, almost every fourth country was involved in an armed conflict. In 2009, that proportion had fallen to every sixth country. In 2050, only every twelfth country will be involved in a conflict. In other words, half as many again. This is indicated by new and sensational conflict simulations by Professor Håvard Hegre of the Department of Political Science at the University of Oslo, conducted in cooperation with the Peace Research Institute Oslo (PRIO).

'The number of conflicts is falling. We expect this fall to continue. We predict a steady fall in the number of conflicts in the next 40 years. Conflicts that involve a high degree of violence, such as Syria, are becoming increasingly rare,' says Hegre.

Great variations

In five years the risk of conflict will be greatest in India, Ethiopia, the Philippines, Uganda and Burma. In 40 years the risk will be greatest in India, Nigeria, Sudan, Ethiopia and Tanzania.

'Those countries in which the risk of conflict will sink most in the next 40 years are Algeria, Colombia, Turkey and Thailand. The conflict level will increase in countries like Tanzania, Mozambique, Malawi and China.

The simulations also show which ongoing conflicts in 2011 will probably be over in five years. These are the conflicts in Libya, Tajikistan, Syria, Senegal, Ivory Coast, Mauritania and Iraq.

The conflict model

'We put a lot of work into developing statistical methods that enable us, with a reasonable degree of certainty, to predict conflicts in the future. A conflict is defined as a conflict between governments and political organisations that use violence and in which at least 25 people die. This means that the model does not cover either tribal wars or solo terrorists like Anders Behring Breivik.'

In the 1700s it was normal to go to war to expand your country's territory.

'This strategy has passed its sell by date. But, demands for democracy may be suppressed with violence and result in more violence in the short term. As in Libya.'

There has been a decrease in armed conflicts and the number of people killed since World War II. This trend will continue.

'War has become less acceptable, just like duelling, torture and the death penalty.'

The conflict model shows that the combination of higher education, lower infant mortality, smaller youth cohorts and lower population growth are a few of the reasons why the world can expect a more peaceful future.

Infant mortality tells us something about socio-economic structure. The UN has calculated infant mortality figures up to 2050.

'Countries with a high infant mortality rate have a high probability of conflict. Infant mortality is now decreasing everywhere.'

The UN has also estimated population structure up to 2050. The population is expected to grow, but at a slower pace than today, and the proportion of young people will decrease in most countries, with the exception of countries in Africa.

The International Institute for Applied Systems Analysis (IIASA) in Vienna has extrapolated the level of education up to 2050.

Too expensive to kill

The simulation model is also based on the last 40 years' history of conflicts, of all countries and their neighbours in the world, oil resources and ethnicity. The conflict data were collated by the Uppsala University.

'Economic changes in society have resulted in both education and human capital becoming important. A complex economy makes political violence less attractive. It has become too expensive to kill people. Modern society is dependent on economic development. It is too expensive to use violence to destroy this network. It has also become harder to take financial capital by force. It is easy to move capital across national borders. Therefore, a cynical leader will be less likely to choose violence as a strategy.'

Education important

It is hard to discern the most important reason why the future will be more peaceful, but some studies suggest that education is the crucial factor.

'Education may be a fundamental causal explanation, but this is difficult to show with our methods. Demographers believe that more education leads to fewer children. There are fewer mouths to feed.'

Another explanation is the UN's peacekeeping operations. The world has become better at employing means of preventing states using violence.

'The UN operations in Bosnia and Somalia failed. But the UN's operations have been more successful since 2000. Of course, the UN cannot prevent conflicts, but fewer die and the intensity is lower when they intervene.'

Wealth in itself, such as oil income, has no positive, economic effect for countries with weak institutions. In some countries, violence is used to control the oil.

Successful test

Hegre used data from 1970 to 2000 to check whether or not the conflict model works as intended. He wanted to see if the model could predict the actual conflicts between 2001 and 2009.

'For 2009 we estimated that the likelihood of a conflict was more than 50 per cent in 20 countries. 16 of these countries ended up in a real conflict. We missed by four countries.'

The simulation program, which for statistical reasons must be run 18,000 times, was programmed by Joakim Karlsen, a research fellow at Østfold University College.

Middle East chaos

The instability in the Middle East impacted the model.

'Prior to the Arabian spring, we expected five per cent of the countries in the world to be involved in a conflict in 2050. This percentage has now risen to seven per cent. The conflicts in the Middle East weaken the clear correlation between socio-economic development and the absence of civil war. The conflicts in Syria and Libya show that we also have to include democratisation processes in the model. To achieve this, we are now working on projecting democratic systems of government and regime changes,' explains Håvard Hegre.

You can read more about this in the scientific article that will soon be published in the periodical *International Studies Quarterly*.

19 November 2012

⇨ The above information is reprinted with kind permission from the University of Oslo. Please visit www.appollon.uio.no for further information.

United Nations Peacekeeping Forces

Background and information about the United Nation Peacekeeping Forces.

By Cara Acred

The United Nations Peacekeeping Forces assist in maintaining, establishing and observing peace in areas of conflict. They provide help and support to countries that are transitioning from a time of war to a time of peace, and to countries that want to avoid the escalation of a conflict.

Operations are divided into unarmed observation missions and lightly armed military forces. All operations are underlined by three core principles:

⇨ Consent of the parties involved – both parties must accept the presence of peacekeeping forces.

⇨ Impartiality – peacekeeping forces have a neutral agenda and do not favour one party over another.

⇨ Non-use of force (except in self-defence or in defence of the mandate).

UN peacekeepers are set apart from other organisations, such as NATO, by their light blue berets/helmets and are often referred to as Blue Helmets.

Currently, there are a total of 15 UN peace operations taking place across four continents:

1948–present
United Nations Truce Supervision Organisation

1949–present
United Nations Military Observer Group in India and Pakistan

1964–present
United Nations Peacekeeping Force in Cyprus

1973–present
Second United Nations Emergency Force

1974–present
United Nations Disengagement Observer Force

1991–present
United Nations Mission for the Referendum in Western Sahara

1999–present
United Nations Interim Administration Mission in Kosovo

2003–present
United Nations Mission in Liberia

2004–present
United Nations Operation in Cote d'Ivoire

2004–present
United Nations Stabilisation Mission in Haiti

2007–present
African Union-United Nations Hybrid Operation in Darfur

2010–present
United Nations Organisation Stabilisation Mission in the Democratic Republic of the Congo

2011–present
United Nations Organisation Interim Security Force for Abyei

2011–present
United Nations Mission in the Republic of South Sudan

2013–present
United Nations Multidimensional Integrated Stabilisation Mission in Malia

Sources:

List of Peacekeeping Operations 1948–2013, United Nations Peacekeeping. Web. 7 Nov 2013. http://www.un.org/en/peacekeeping/documents/operationslist.pdf

What is peacekeeping? United Nations Peacekeeping. Web. 7 Nov 2013. http://www.un.org/en/peacekeeping/operations/peacekeeping.shtml

United Nations Peacekeeping Forces – History. Nobelprize.org. Nobel Media AB 2013. Web. 7 Nov 2013. http://www.nobelprize.org/nobel_prizes/peace/laureates/1988/un-history.html

Making Misrata safer with MAG: clearing unexploded ordnance in Libya

How a British charity is helping communities recover from conflict.

A year ago, Libya was in throes of a violent conflict. Now, a fragile peace and normality is beginning to return. 15-year-old children like Mohamed can play with a football in the streets of Misrata again.

But Mohamed was playing with something much more dangerous this time last year – part of a rifle grenade that had landed near his house. He picked it up off the street thinking it was safe, but it exploded in his bedroom. He lost most of his left hand.

Mohamed is one of a growing number of people in Libya who have fallen victim to unexploded ordnance (UXO) – grenades, land mines, rockets and ammunition – all grim remnants of the conflict which gripped the country for much of 2011.

High levels of abandoned and dangerous UXO still litter the towns and roads where fighting took place. Without professional disposal and adequate understanding of the dangers many people, especially children, remain at risk of serious harm.

'Children are particularly attracted to 23mm bullets as they are in abundance and easy to pick up,' said Alexandra Arango, who works as a Community Liaison Manager for British charity MAG (Mines Awareness Group), who specialise in clearing land mines and other UXO in former conflict zones around the world.

'Most children play with them for a while until they decide to throw rocks at them or tap them onto a surface and they explode, injuring their hand and causing shrapnel injuries on their chest or face.'

With support from the UK Government and other donors, MAG began working in Libya last April, to carry out initial assessments, before establishing operations in May to conduct Explosive Ordnance Disposal around the coastal area of Ajdabiya, Brega and Misrata.

Key to MAG's work has also been the development of Physical Security and Stockpile Management (PSSM) operations. PSSM makes safe the leftover weapons and munitions, preventing them falling into the wrong hands.

MAG have also established Community Focal Points (CFPs) – groups made up of a representative range of men, women and young people – in the most contaminated areas in and around Zintan. The CFPs deliver targeted risk education and also help gather information on dangerous areas. This assists clearance operations, ensuring that MAG focuses their resources in the areas where the need is greatest.

More than 48,000 people have so far benefited directly or indirectly from MAG's Risk Education work.

MAG disposal teams have destroyed more than 100,000 remnants of conflict, including anti-personnel landmines, anti-tank mines, cluster submunitions, UXO items and small arms ammunition. MAG has cleared nine schools in and around Ajdabiya and Brega, and seven in Misrata, as well as houses, roads and other public areas.

They have recorded 8,275 direct beneficiaries from clearance, and more than 350,000 indirect beneficiaries, in Misrata, Ajdabiya, Brega and Benghazi.

Mohamed's father, Abdul said: 'Everyone in this area knows about this accident and everyone now tells their children not to touch these things. We didn't know before but we certainly do now'.

There is still much to do before Libya becomes safe enough for communities to develop and thrive socially and economically.

Until then, MAG's clearance and risk education operations will continue to work towards creating a platform for peace and stability, supporting wider humanitarian and post-conflict reconstruction efforts.

4 April 2012

⇨ The above information is reprinted with kind permission from the Department for International Development. Please visit www.gov.uk for further information.

Key facts

- Conflict in Afghanistan has resulted in death and injury to thousands of civilians. (page 1)

- In 2006, a majority of states voted at the UN General Assembly to consider the question of a universal and legally binding Arms Trade Treaty. (page 2)

- The Uppsala University's Conflict Data Program registered 32 armed conflicts in 2012, and 37 in 2011. (page 6)

- Despite the number of armed conflicts decreasing in 2012, the number of battle-related deaths increased. (page 6)

- The conflict in Syria is the bloodiest since the war between Eritrea and Ethiopia in 1999-2001. (page 6)

- Over 75 countries and territories around the world are affected by landmines and/or explosive remnants of war. (page 9)

- More than 360 models of landmines have been manufactured. (page 9)

- A fixed directional effect mine has the potential to cause serious or fatal injuries over a distance of up to 50 metres. (page 9)

- In the mid-2000s, Britain guaranteed £178 million of loans to Iran to buy British exports for gas and oil developments. (page 11)

- The highest ranking arms producing and military services company in the world, 2010, is Lockheed Martin. (page 17)

- By the end of 2004, some 3.3 million people were displaced within Asia-Pacific regions due to conflicts. (page 18)

- About half of the 2.1 million Internally Displaced Persons from the Middle East, have been displaced for two decades or longer. (page 18)

- 61% of the British public would oppose the British Government sending full-scale military supplies to the anti-Assaad troops in Syria. (page 21)

- In 2010, the estimated number of asylum applications in 44 industrialised countries was 358,800. (page 23)

- Since 2010, child soldier use by 20 states has been reported in government-armed forces or indirectly in armed groups which they support or are allied to. (page 24)

- In just 22 days, from 27th December 2008 to 18th January 2009, 350 children were killed and 1,815 were injured in the Israeli military attack on Gaza. (page 25)

- In 1992, almost every fourth country was involved in an armed conflict. In 2009, that proportion had fallen to every sixth country. (page 36)

- Simulations show that ongoing conflicts in 2011 will be over in five years. (page 36)

- Currently, there are a total of 15 UN peace operations taking place throughout the world. (page 38)

- More than 48,000 people so far have benefited directly or indirectly from MAG's Risk Education work. (page 39)

Arms Trade Treaty (ATT)

The purpose of the Arms Trade Treaty (ATT) is to monitor and control the trading of weapons (arms) more closely; ensuring that weapons are traded more responsibly and preventing arms being supplied to people who abuse human right law.

The aim of the ATT is to help prevent the irresponsible trade in arms, save lives and reduce the suffering of millions affected by war and armed violence.

Chemical weapons

Weapons that use deadly chemicals to hurt, maim and kill their targets. These chemicals can be in the form of a gas, a liquid or a solid and can be used over a wide area.

During the First World War a poisonous gas called mustard gas caused large blisters on exposed skin and in the lungs. A modern example of a chemical weapon is tear gas, which is a non-poisonous gas and has no deadly effects but can cause pain to the eyes and temporary blindness.

Drone

A remote-controlled aircraft without a pilot. Usually used to observe an area (e.g. surveillance drone), but can be armed with missiles. The use of unmanned surveillance drones is controversial; on one hand they can map areas far quicker than a human could, but conversely they can breach human privacy rights.

Humanitarian Intervention

When a state uses military force against another state whose military action is violating citizens' human rights. For example, the British Government recently questioned whether they should send the British Armed Forced to intervene and stop the human rights violations in Syria.

Immigrant

A person who moves permanently from their home country and settles somewhere else that is foreign to them. They may leave their home country for a number of reasons, for example to seek better job opportunities abroad or even because they have been forced to leave to escape conflict in their home country.

Internal conflict

Conflict that takes place within a state, between government forces and one or more organised groups. Or between these groups themselves.

Internal displacement

When people are forced to flee – whether due to natural disasters, chemical/nuclear disasters, famine, development projects or conflict – and remain within the borders of their country.

International human rights law

International humanitarian law (IHL) is a set of rules which seek to protect people who are not participating in armed conflict, like civilians and wounded, sick or shipwrecked members of the armed forces. It also restricts the means and methods of warfare. Also known as the law of war or the law of armed conflict, the best known of these rules are the four Geneva Conventions of 1949.

Landmine

An explosive device that is hidden just beneath the ground and goes off when someone passes near or over the device. Landmines have been increasingly used around the world because they do not cost much to make yet they cause a lot of damage. They can remain hidden for years or even decades, which poses a risk to civilians or aid workers long after a conflict has ended.

Nuclear weapon

An explosive device that has enormous destructive power and releases a vast amount of energy. Even a small nuclear weapon has the power to wipe out a city. Also known as Weapons of Mass Destruction (WMD)

Peacekeeping

Actively maintaining peaceful relations between nations.

Refugee

A person who is seeking a place of safety. A refugee moves away from the country of their birth and are unwilling or unable to return because it is too dangerous.

Responsibility to Protect

The Responsibility to Protect (RtoP or R2P) is in place to prevent and stop genocide, war crimes, ethnic cleansing and crimes against humanity. The Responsibility to Protect is not a law, but rather a political commitment to guide states in protecting populations from these crimes and violations.

War

Armed conflict between different countries/groups/states.

Assignments

Brainstorming

⇨ In small groups, brainstorm and create a poster that demonstrates everything you know about war and conflict. You should consider the following questions:

- What are some of the triggers or reasons behind war and conflict?

- What kind of weapons are used in modern warfare?

- What do different religions think of the concept of war?

- What are some of the effects of war?

Research

⇨ Find an example of Internal Conflict. Create a PowerPoint presentation explaining the main reasons behind the conflict, how it has escalated and how the conflict is being/was dealt with.

⇨ Read the article on page 3 *World religions: war and peace*. Choose one religion and research their views on war and peace. Create a leaflet that demonstrates your findings.

⇨ Look at the map on page 6 and choose an area of 'serious' or 'high' conflict. Find out which episodes of political violence have occurred in your chosen area since 1946. Create a table that lists the parties/countries involved, the cause, the date the conflict started and the date it ended.

⇨ Look at the table on page 17 and choose one of the top ten arms-producing and military services companies in the world. Research this company and find out what they produce, how big they are and where their offices are located. Feedback to your class.

⇨ Choose a historical conflict, such as World War II, and research the kind of weapons that were used. Write a short summary.

⇨ Choose one of the United Nations Peacekeeping Operations listed on page 38 and research it further. Write a summary of your findings.

Design

⇨ Create a poster that explains International Humanitarian Law.

⇨ Create a poster campaign that will draw attention to the issue of Child Soldiers.

⇨ Read the article *United Nation Peacekeeping Forces* on page 38 and design a leaflet which explains why peacekeeping is important and what is involved.

Oral

⇨ Read the article on page 3 *World religions: war and peace*. As a class, stage a debate in which half of you argue that all violence and killing is wrong (pacifist) and the other half argue that some wars are 'just'.

⇨ Choose one of the illustrations from the book and discuss it with a friend. What do you think the artist was trying to portray? Do you think they have succeeded?

⇨ Imagine you work for a charity that campaigns against the use of landmines. Prepare a five-minute talk to perform in front of your class, highlighting the dangers and effects of landmines.

⇨ In pairs, discuss whether you think that drones and robots should be banned. Are there positive things that they could be used for? What are the risks involved?

⇨ In pairs discuss whether you think that humanitarian intervention is justified.

⇨ Create a short presentation, explaining the current conflict in Syria.

⇨ In small groups, discuss what you would do if you were a political party trying to bring about world peace.

Reading/writing

⇨ Write a definition of Internal Displacement.

⇨ Choose one of the case studies from the article on page 33 *Establishing stability in Afghanistan* and write a short news article about it.

⇨ Do some research into the daily lives of women in Afghanistan then write a blog post from the perspective of one of these women.

⇨ Imagine it is the year 3000 and that the world is living in peace. Write a short story, 600–1,000 words, about what the world is like.

⇨ How would you explain war to a class of younger students? In groups, create a lesson plan that you could use with ten- to 12-year-old students.

Acknowledgements

The publisher is grateful for permission to reproduce the material in this book. While every care has been taken to trace and acknowledge copyright, the publisher tenders its apology for any accidental infringement or where copyright has proved untraceable. The publisher would be pleased to come to a suitable arrangement in any such case with the rightful owner.

Images

Cover, page iii and page 2: iStock, page 1 © Expert Infantry, page 9 © Cluster Munition Coalition, Page 14: iStock, page 18 © EU Humanitarian Aid and Intervention, page 25 © Julien Harneis, page 27 © Philippe AMIOT, page 32 © The US Army, page 39 © Foreign and Commonwealth Office.

Illustrations

Page 4: Angelo Madrid, page 5: Angelo Madrid, page 12: Don Hatcher, page 16: Simon Kneebone, page 29: Don Hatcher, page 37: Simon Kneebone.

Additional acknowledgements

Editorial on behalf of Independence Educational Publishers by Cara Acred.

With thanks to the Independence team: Mary Chapman, Sandra Dennis, Christina Hughes, Jackie Staines and Jan Sunderland.

Cara Acred

Cambridge, January 2014